Collins Complete Outdoor DIY

Collins complete outdoor DIY

Albert Jackson and David Day

Collins

Collins Complete Outdoor DIY
was originally created for HarperCollins Publishers by
Inklink/Jackson Day Jennings. Most of the material in
this book also appears in *Collins Complete DIY Manual*.

This first edition first published in 2008 by
Collins, an imprint of
HarperCollinsPublishers
77-85 Fulham Palace Road
Hammersmith
London W6 8JB

Collins is a registered trademark
of HarperCollins Publishers Ltd

13   12   11   10   09   08
6   5   4   3   2   1

A catalogue record for this book is available from
The British Library

ISBN 978 000 726671 5

Colour reproduction by Colourscan, Singapore
Printed and bound by Printing Express, Hong Kong

PLEASE NOTE
**Great care has been taken to ensure that the
information contained in Collins Complete Outdoor DIY
is accurate. However, the law concerning Building
Regulations, planning, local bylaws and
related matters is neither static nor simple. A book
of this nature cannot replace specialist advice in
appropriate cases and therefore no responsibility
can be accepted by the publishers or by the authors
for any loss or damage caused by reliance upon the
accuracy of such information.**

**If you live outside Britain, your local conditions
may mean that some of this information is not
appropriate. If in doubt, always consult a qualified
electrician, plumber or surveyor.**

Authors
Albert Jackson and David Day

Photographers
Airedale/David Murphy
Colin Bowling
Paul Chave
Ben Jennings
Neil Waving

Design
Elizabeth Standley

New Illustrations
Graham White

Illustrations
Robin Harris
John Pinder

Editors
Peter Leek

Proofreader and Indexer
Mary Morton

Acknowledgements
The authors and publishers would like to thank the following
companies and individuals who supplied images or tools for
photography:

6 John Glover/The Garden Picture Library, Simon Jennings;
7 Henry Dijkman/The Garden Picture Library, Simon Jennings,
Clay Perry/The Garden Picture Library, Ron Sutherland/
The Garden Picture Library; 8 Marshalls Mono Ltd; 9 Simon
Jennings, Alan Marshall; 10 Simon Jennings; 11Simon Jennings;
17 Simon Jennings; 18 Simon Jennings; 19 Simon Jennings;
20 Simon Jennings; 22 Simon Jennings; 24 Bradstone
Aggregate Industries Ltd, Albert Jackson, Simon Jennings,
Marshalls Mono Ltd; 26 Simon Jennings; 33 Simon Jennings;
35 Simon Jennings; 36 Simon Jennings; 37 Rodney
Hyett/Elizabeth Whiting Associates, Simon Jennings,
Marshalls Mono Ltd; 39 Mixamate; 43 Wickes Building
Supplies Ltd; 45 Cement and Concrete Association, Ronseal
Ltd; 46 Barlow Tyrie Ltd, Marshalls Mono Ltd; 48 Forest Garden
Plc, Simon Jennings, Marshalls Mono Ltd; 49 Forest Garden
Plc, Marshalls Mono Ltd; 50 Liberon Ltd; 51 Simon Jennings,
Marshalls Mono Ltd; 52 Marshalls Mono Ltd; 54 Lotus Water
Gardens; 55 Simon Jennings; 56 Albert Jackson, Stapeley
Gardens; 57 Stapeley Gardens; 60 Marshalls Mono Ltd;
62 David Day; 64–67 Axminster Power Tool Centre, Draper
Tools, L.G Harris, Irwin Tools, Jewson, Monument Tools,
Plasplugs, Screwfix, Wolfcraft

Contents

Working
Outdoors

Reference

Planning a garden

Designing a garden is not an exact science. You may, for example, find that plants don't thrive, even though you have selected species that are recommended for your soil conditions. And trees don't always conform to the size specified in a catalogue. Nevertheless, forward planning can avert some of the more unfortunate mistakes, such as laying a patio where it will be in shade for most of the day, or digging a fish pond that's too small to create the required conditions for fish. Concentrate on planning the more permanent features first, taking into consideration how they will affect the planted areas of your garden.

Getting inspired

There's no shortage of material from which you can draw inspiration – there are countless books, magazines and TV programmes devoted to garden planning. But, as no two gardens are alike, you probably won't find a plan that fits your plot exactly. However, you may be able to adapt a design to suit your needs or integrate some eye-catching details into your scheme.

Visiting real gardens is even better. Although large country estates and city parks are designed on a grand scale, you will be able to see how mature shrubs should look or how plants, stone and water can be used in a rockery or water garden.

Some towns and city boroughs host 'open days', when members of the public extend an invitation to anyone who wants to look around their gardens. Don't forget that friends and neighbours may have had to tackle problems similar to your own – and if nothing else, you may learn from their mistakes!

The approach

Before you put pencil to paper, think about the type of garden you want, and ask yourself whether it will sit happily with your house and its surroundings. Is it to be a formal garden, laid out in straight lines and geometric patterns – a style that often marries successfully with modern houses? Or do you prefer the more relaxed style of a rambling cottage garden? If you opt for the latter, remember that natural informality may not be as easy to achieve as you think, and your planting scheme will probably take years to mature into the garden you have in mind. Or maybe you're attracted to the idea of a Japanese-style garden – in effect a blend of both these styles, with every plant, stone and pool of water carefully positioned, so that the garden bears all the hallmarks of a man-made landscape and yet conveys a sense of natural harmony.

Consider the details
Period-style cast ornaments that add character to a garden need not cost a fortune.

Juxtaposing textures
Create eye-catching focal points, using well-considered combinations of natural form and texture.

Planning on a small scale
Good garden design does not rely on having a large plot of land. Here, curvilinear shapes draw the eye through a delightful array of foliage and flowers planted around a beautifully manicured lawn and a small but perfectly balanced fish pond.

SEE ALSO > Planning in more detail 8

Surveying the plot

In order to make the best use of your plot of land, you need to take fairly accurate measurements and check the prevailing conditions.

Measuring up

Make a note of the overall dimensions of your plot. At the same time, check the diagonal measurements – because your garden may not be the perfect rectangle or square it appears to be. The diagonals are especially important when plotting irregular shapes.

Slopes and gradients

Check how the ground slopes. You don't need an accurate survey, but at least jot down the direction of the slope and plot the points where the gradient begins and ends. You can get some idea of the differences in level by using a long straightedge and a spirit level. Place one end of the straightedge on the top of a bank, for example, and measure the vertical distance from the other end to the foot of the slope.

Keep any useful features

Plot the position of existing features, such as pathways, areas of lawn and established trees.

How about the weather?

Check the passage of the sun and the direction of prevailing winds. Don't forget that the angle of the sun will be higher in summer, and that a screen of deciduous trees will be less effective as a windbreak when the leaves drop.

Soil conditions

The type of soil you have in your garden is bound to influence your choice of plants, but you can easily adjust soil content by adding peat or fertilizers. Clay soil, which is greyish in colour, is heavy when wet and tends to crack when dry. A sandy soil feels gritty and loose in dry conditions. Acidic peat soil is dark brown and flaky. Pale-coloured chalky soil, which often contains flints, will not support acid-loving plants. Any soil that contains too many stones or too much gravel is unsuitable as topsoil.

Measuring a plot
To draw an accurate plan, note down the overall dimensions, including the diagonals.

Irregular plot

Corner plot

Gauging a slope
Use a straightedge and spirit level to measure the height of a bank.

Theme gardens
Deciding on a style or theme for your garden will help you with the overall planning right from the start. The very different themes shown here are examples of the seemingly random planting of a colourful cottage garden, the pleasing symmetry of formal layouts, and the 'natural' informality of a Japanese-style garden carefully constructed from selected rocks, pebbles and sculptural foliage.

SEE ALSO > Planning in more detail 8, Creating a water garden 56

Planning in more detail

Armed with all the measurements you've taken, make a simple drawing to try out your ideas. Then, to make sure your plan will work in reality, mark out the shapes and plot the important features in your garden.

Drawing a plan on paper

Draw a plan of your garden on paper. It must be a properly scaled plan, or you are sure to make some gross errors - but it need not be professionally perfect. Use squared graph paper to plot the garden's dimensions and any relevant features - but do the actual drawing on tracing paper laid over the grid, so you can try out different ideas and makes alterations to your plan without having to redraw it each time.

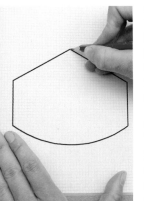

Drawing plans
Draw a garden plan on tracing paper laid over squared graph paper.

Plotting your design on the ground

Planning on paper is only the first stage. Gardens are rarely seen from above, so it is essential to plot the design on the ground to check your dimensions and view the features from different angles.

A pond or patio that seems enormous on paper may look pathetically small in reality. Other shortcomings, such as the way a tree will block the view from your proposed patio, become obvious once you lay out the plan full size.

Plot individual features - such as a patio or a raised flower bed - by driving pegs into the ground and stretching string lines between them.

Use a rope tied to a peg to scribe arcs on the ground, and mark the curved lines with stakes or a row of bricks.

A garden hose provides the ideal aid for marking out less regular curves. If you can scrape areas clear of weeds, that will define the shapes still further.

Mark out straight lines with pegs and string

Use rope tied to a peg to scribe an arc

Practical experiments

When you have marked out your design, carry out a few experiments to check that it is practicable.

Will it be possible, for instance, for two people to pass each other on the garden path without having to step into the flowerbeds? Can you set down a wheelbarrow on the path without one of its legs slipping into the pond?

Try placing some furniture on the area you have marked out for your patio to make sure there is enough room to relax comfortably and sit down to a meal with visitors. Most people build a patio along-side the house, but if you have to put it elsewhere to find a sunny spot, will it become a chore to walk to and fro with drinks and snacks?

Siting a pond
Position a pond to avoid overhanging trees, and in an area where it will catch at least half a day's sunlight. Check that you can reach it with a hose and that you can run electrical cables to power a pump or lighting.

Common-sense safety
Don't make your garden an obstacle course. A narrow path alongside a pond, for example, may be hazardous or intimidating for an elderly relative; and low walls or planters near the edge of a patio could cause someone to trip.

Driveways and parking spaces
Allow a minimum width of 3m (9ft 9in) for a driveway, making sure there is enough room to open the doors of a car parked alongside a wall. And bear in mind that vehicles larger than your own might need to use the drive or parking space. If possible, allow room for the turning circle of your car; and make sure you will have a clear view of the traffic when you pull out into the road.

Plotting curved features
Use rope tied to a peg to lay out circles and arcs on the ground.

Try out irregular curves with a garden hose

Don't neglect your neighbours

There are legal restrictions regarding what you can erect in your garden. However, even if you have a free hand, it's worth consulting your neighbours in case anything you're planning might inconvenience them. A wall or row of trees that throws shade across a neighbour's patio or blocks the light to their windows could be the source of a bitter dispute lasting for years.

Make sure two people can pass easily on a path

SEE ALSO > Constructing ponds 56–62, Pumps and fountains 60

Growing climbers

There's a widely held belief that climbing plants, especially ivy, will damage any masonry wall.

If exterior rendering or the mortar between bricks or stonework is in poor condition, then a vigorous ivy plant will undoubtedly weaken the structure as its aerial roots attempt to extract moisture from the masonry. The roots will invade broken joints or rendering and, on finding a source of nourishment for the main plant, expand and burst the weakened material. This encourages damp to penetrate the wall.

Don't allow climbers to get out of control

However, when clinging to sound masonry, ivy can do no more than climb with the aid of training wires and its own sucker-like roots that do not provide nourishment but are for support only.

So long as the structure is sound and free from damp, there is even some benefit in allowing a plant to clothe a wall, since its close-growing mat of leaves, mostly with their drip tips pointing downwards, acts as insulation and provides some protection against the elements.

Climbers must be pruned regularly, so they don't penetrate between roof tiles or slates, or clog gutters and drain-pipes. If a robust climber is allowed to grow unchecked, the weight of the mature plant may eventually topple a weakened wall.

Training wires
Climbing plants can be controlled by fixing horizontal wires at the required height.

Trees and foundations

When planning your garden, you will probably want to include some trees. However, you should think carefully about your choice of trees and their position – they could be potentially damaging to the structure of your house if planted too near to it.

Siting trees

Tree roots searching for moisture can do considerable harm to a drainage system, fracturing rigid pipework and penetrating joints, eventually blocking the drain.

Before planting a tree close to the house, find out how far its root system is likely to spread. Estimate its likely maximum height, and take this as a guide as to how far from the house you should plant the tree.

If you think an existing tree is likely to cause problems, don't be tempted to chop it down without first consulting your local planning department – some trees are protected by preservation orders and you could be fined if you cut down a protected tree without permission. A professional tree surgeon may be able to solve the problem by pruning its roots and branches.

Minor cracks in plaster and rendering are often the result of shrinkage as the structure dries out. Such cracks are not serious and can be repaired during normal maintenance, but more serious structural cracks are due to movement of the foundations. Trees planted too close to a building can add to the problem by removing moisture from the site, causing subsidence of the foundations as the supporting earth collapses. But tree felling can be just as damaging – the surrounding soil, which has stabilized over the years, swells as it takes up the moisture that was previously removed by the tree's root system. As a result, upward movement of the ground – known as heave – distorts the foundations, and cracks begin to appear.

Subsidence
A mature tree growing close to a house can draw so much water from the ground that the earth subsides, causing damage to the foundations.

Heave
When a mature tree is felled, the earth can absorb more water, causing it to swell until it displaces the foundations of the building.

SEE ALSO > Planning a garden 6

Choosing fences

A fence is a popular form of boundary marker or garden screen, primarily because it is relatively inexpensive and takes very little time to erect. In the short term a fence is cheaper than a masonry wall, although one can argue that the cost of maintenance and replacement over a long period eventually cancels out the saving in cost. Wood has a comparatively short life, because it is susceptible to insect infestation and rot, but a fence can last for years if it's treated regularly with a preserver. And if you choose plastic or concrete components, then your fence will be virtually maintenance-free.

Talk to your neighbours

Discuss your plans with your neighbours, especially as you will require their permission if you want to work from both sides of the boundary when erecting the fence. Check the exact line of the boundary to make certain that you don't encroach upon your neighbour's land. The fence posts should run along the boundary or on your side of the line – and before you dismantle an old fence, make sure it is indeed yours to demolish.

If a neighbour is unwilling to replace an unsightly fence and won't even allow you to replace it at your expense, there is nothing to stop you erecting another fence alongside the original one – provided that it's on your property.

Although it is an unwritten law that a good neighbour erects a fence with the post and rails facing his or her own property, there are no legal restrictions that could force you to do so.

Natural-log fencing
Construct your own informal fencing using split logs nailed to horizontal rails.

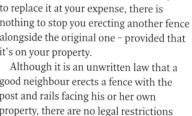

Chain-link fencing

Trellis fencing

Post-and-chain fencing

Planning permission

As a rule, you can build any fence up to 2m (6ft 6in) high without having to obtain planning permission. However, if your boundary adjoins a highway, you may not be allowed to erect any barrier higher than 1m (3ft 3in). In addition, there could be restrictions on fencing if the land surrounding your house has been designed as an open-plan area. Even so, many authorities will permit you to erect low boundary markers such as ranch-style or post-and-chain fencing.

You may be surprised by how much fencing you need to surround even a small garden – so it's worth considering the available options carefully, to make sure you invest your money in a fence that will meet your needs. Unless your priority is to keep neighbourhood children or animals out of your garden, privacy is most likely to be the prime consideration. There are a number of 'peep-proof' options, but you may have to compromise to some extent if you plan to erect a fence on a site exposed to strong prevailing winds. In this situation, you will need a fence that will act as a windbreak without offering so much resistance that the posts work loose within a couple of seasons.

Chain-link fencing

Consisting of wire netting stretched between posts, chain-link fencing is purely functional. It is made from strong galvanized or plastic-coated wire mesh that is suspended from a heavy-gauge cable, known as a straining wire, strung between the posts. Decorative wire fencing, which is available at many garden centres, is designed primarily for marking boundaries or supporting lightweight climbing plants. Except in a remote rural location, any chain-link fence will benefit from a screen of climbers or hedging plants.

SEE ALSO > Fence posts 12–13, Erecting fencing 13–17

Trellis fencing

Concertina-fold trellis constructed from thin softwood or from cedar laths is designed primarily to help plants climb a wall, but rigid panels made from softwood battens can be used in conjunction with fence posts to erect a substantial free-standing screen. Most garden centres stock a wide range of these decorative panels. A similar fence made from split rustic poles nailed to stout rails and posts forms a strong and attractive barrier.

Post-and-chain fencing

A post-and-chain fence is no more than a decorative feature intended to prevent people from inadvertently wandering off a path or pavement onto a lawn or flower-bed. This type of fencing is constructed by stringing lengths of painted metal or plastic chain between short posts sunk into the ground.

Closeboard fencing

A closeboard fence is made by nailing overlapping featherboard strips to horizontal rails. Featherboards are sawn planks that taper across their width, from 16mm (⅝in) at the thicker edge down to about 3mm (⅛in). The boards are usually 100mm (4in) or 150mm (6in) wide. The best-quality featherboards are made from cedar, but softwood is the usual choice in view of the amount of timber required to make a long closeboard fence. Although it is expensive, closeboard fencing forms a screen that is both strong and attractive. Being fixed vertically, the boards make a high fence quite difficult to climb from the outside – which makes them ideal for keeping intruders out.

Prefabricated panel fencing

Fences made from prefabricated panels nailed between timber posts are very popular, perhaps because they are so easy to erect. Standard fence panels are 1.8m (6ft) wide and range in height from 600mm (2ft) to 1.8m (6ft); they are supplied in 300mm (1ft) gradations.

Most prefabricated fence panels are made from interwoven or overlapping strips of wood sandwiched between a frame of sawn timber.

Overlapping-strip panels are usually designated as 'lap' or 'larchlap'. When the strips have a natural wavy edge, they are sometimes called 'rustic' or 'waney' lap.

Any panel fence tends to be good value for money and will provide durable screening – but if privacy is a consideration choose the lapped type, as interwoven strips can shrink in the summer, leaving gaps in the fence.

Interlap fencing

An interlap fence is made by nailing square-edged boards to horizontal rails, fixing the boards alternately on one side, then the other. Spacing is a matter of choice – you can overlap the edges of the boards for privacy, or space them apart to create a more decorative effect. This type of fencing is a sensible choice for a windy site. Although it's a sturdy screen, it permits a strong wind to pass through the gaps between the boards, reducing the amount of pressure exerted on the fence. Being equally attractive from either side, an interlap fence is perfect as boundary screening.

Picket fencing

The traditional low picket fence is still popular as a 'cottage-style' barrier at the front of the house, particularly where a high fence would look out of place. Narrow, vertical 'pales' with rounded or pointed tops are spaced at about 75 to 100mm (3 to 4in) centres. As they are laborious to build by hand, to keep down the cost most picket fences are sold as ready-made panels constructed from plastic or softwood.

Ranch-style fencing

Low-level fences made from simple horizontal rails fixed to short, stout posts are the modern counterpart of picket fencing. Used to divide up building plots in some housing developments, ranch-style fencing is often painted, although clear-finished or stained timber is just as attractive and much more durable. Softwood and some hardwoods are commonplace materials for this kind of fencing, but plastic ranch-style fences are also popular because of their clean, crisp appearance and also because there's no need to repaint them and there is very little maintenance.

Concrete fencing

A cast-concrete fence is maintenance-free, and it provides the same security and permanence as a wall built from brick or stone. Interlocking horizontal sections are built one upon the other, up to the required height. Each vertical stack is supported by grooves cast into the sides of purpose-made concrete fence posts. This relatively heavy fencing would be dangerous if the posts were not firmly embedded in concrete.

Closeboard fencing

Panel fence

Interlap fencing

Picket fencing

Ranch-style fence

Concrete fencing

SEE ALSO > Fence posts 12–13, Erecting fencing 13–17

Fence posts

Whatever type of fence you decide to erect, its strength and durability will rely on good-quality posts set solidly in the ground. Erecting the posts carefully and accurately is crucial to the longevity of the fence and may save you having to either re-erect or repair it in the future.

Capping fence posts
If you simply cut the end of a timber post square, the top of the post will rot relatively quickly. The solution is to cut a single or double bevel to shed the rainwater, or nail a cap made from wood or galvanized metal over the end of the post.

Choosing fence posts

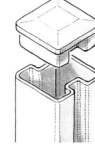

Square timber post

Capped plastic post

Angle-iron post

Tubular-steel post

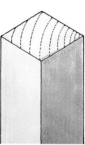

Drilled concrete post

Mortised concrete post

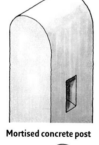

Grooved concrete post

Notched end post

In some cases, the nature of the fencing will determine the choice of post. Concrete fencing, for example, has to be supported by compatible concrete posts. But in the main you can choose the material and style of post that suits the appearance of the fence.

Timber posts
Most fences are supported by square-section timber posts. Standard fence-post sizes are 75 or 100mm (3 or 4in) square, but gateposts 125, 150 and even 200mm (5, 6 and 8in) square are available. Unless you ask specifically for hardwood, most timber merchants will supply you with pretreated softwood posts.

Plastic posts
Extruded PVC posts are supplied with plastic fencing, together with moulded-plastic end caps and rail-fixing bolts and unions.

Metal posts
Angle-iron posts are made to support chain-link fences; and wrought-iron gates are often hung from plastic-coated tubular-steel posts. Angle-iron posts are very sturdy, but they do not make an attractive fence.

Concrete posts
A variety of reinforced-concrete posts, 100mm (4in) square, are produced to suit different styles of fence – drilled for chain-link fixings, mortised for rails, and recessed or grooved for panels. Special corner and end posts (see opposite) are notched to accommodate bracing struts for chain-link fencing.

Preserving fence posts

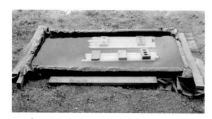

Even when a timber fence post is pretreated to prevent rot, you can make doubly sure by soaking the base of each post in a bucket of chemical preserver overnight.

Untreated timber needs to be immersed for a similar period in a polythene-lined trough filled with preserver.

Fixing to a wall

If a fence runs up to the house, fix the first post to the wall, using three expanding masonry bolts. Place a washer under each bolt head to stop the wood being crushed. Check that the post is vertical and, if need be, drive packing between the post and wall to make adjustments.

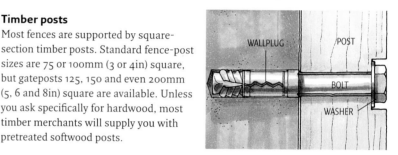

WALLPLUG   POST

BOLT

WASHER

Bolting a post to a wall
If you are fitting a prefabricated panel against a wall-fixed post, counterbore the bolts so that the heads lie flush with the surface of the wood.

Removing old posts

If you are replacing a dilapidated fence, it may prove convenient to put the new posts in the same position as the old.

Begin by dismantling the featherboards and rails, or cut through the fixings so you can remove the fence panels. If any of the posts are bedded firmly or sunk into concrete, you will have to lever them out with a stout batten. Remove the topsoil from around each post to loosen it. Drive large nails into two opposite faces of the post, about 300mm (1ft) from the ground. Bind a length of rope around the post, just below the nails, and tie the ends to the tip of the batten. Build a pile of bricks close to the post, and use it as a fulcrum to lever the post out of the ground.

SEE ALSO > Erecting fence posts 13

Erecting fence posts

The type of fence you choose dictates whether you need to erect all the posts first or put them up one at a time, along with the other components. If you are building a prefabricated panel fence, for example, fix the posts as you erect the fence; but if you're putting up chain-link fencing, complete the run of posts first.

Marking out a row of fence posts

Drive a peg into the ground at each end of the fence run, and stretch a length of string between the pegs to align the row of posts. If possible, adjust the spacing to avoid obstructions such as large tree roots. If one or more posts have to be inserted across a paved patio, either lift enough slabs to allow you to dig the required holes or mark out the patio for bolt-down metal post sockets (see right).

Erecting the posts

Bury one quarter of each post. You can hire post-hole augers to remove the central core of earth. Twist the tool to drive it into the ground (**1**) and pull it out after every 150mm (6in) to remove the soil. When you have reached a sufficient depth, taper the sides of the hole slightly so that you can pack hardcore around the post.

Anchoring the post
Ram a layer of hardcore (broken bricks or small stones) into the bottom of the hole to support the base of the post and provide drainage. Get someone to hold the post upright while you brace it with battens nailed to the post and to stakes driven into the ground. Use guy ropes to support a concrete post. Check with a spirit level that the post is vertical (**2**).

Ram some more hardcore around the post, leaving a hole about 300mm (1ft) deep for filling with concrete. Top up with a fast-setting concrete mix made specially for erecting fence posts. Alternatively, mix some general-purpose concrete and tamp it into the hole with the end of a batten (**3**). Build the concrete just above the level of the soil and smooth it to slope away from the post. This will help shed rainwater and prevent rot.

Leave the concrete to harden before removing the struts. Support a panel fence temporarily, with struts wedged against the posts.

1 Dig the post hole

2 Brace the post

3 Tamp the concrete

Supporting end posts

Chain-link fence posts must resist the tension of the straining wires. Brace each end post (and some of the intermediate ones over a long run) with a strut made from a length of fence post. Shape the end of the strut to fit a notch cut into the post and nail it in place. You can order special precast concrete end posts and struts. Anchor the post in the ground and dig a trench 450mm (1ft 6in) deep alongside for the strut. Wedge a brick under the end of the strut, then ram hardcore around the post and strut. Fill the trench up to ground level with concrete. Support a corner post with two struts at right angles.

Braced end post

Using metal sockets

Instead of digging holes for your fence posts, you can plug the base of each post into a square socket attached to a metal spike that is driven into firm ground. Similar sockets can be bolted to existing paving or set in fresh concrete.

Use 600mm (2ft) spikes for fences up to 1.2m (4ft) high, and 750mm (2ft 6in) spikes for a 1.8m (6ft) fence. Place a proprietary driving tool into the socket to protect the metal and then drive the spike partly into the ground with a sledgehammer.

Hold a spirit level against the socket to make certain the spike is upright (**1**), then hammer the spike into the ground until only the socket is visible. Insert the post and, depending on the type of spike, secure it by screwing through the side of the socket or by tightening clamping bolts (**2**). If you're putting up a panel fence, use the edge of a fixed panel to position the next spike.

Fence-post spikes

Bolted sockets
Bolt this type of socket to existing patios and concrete driveways.

Embedded sockets
Embed this type of socket in wet concrete.

1 Use a level to check the spike is vertical

2 Tighten the bolts to clamp the post

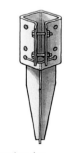

Repair socket
Allows replacement of rotten or broken posts set in concrete. Cut off the old post flush with the concrete and then drive the spike into the centre of the stump.

SEE ALSO > Chain-link fencing 10, Intermediate posts 14, Straining wires 14, Erecting a panel fence 16, Mixing concrete 39

Putting up chain-link fencing

To support chain-link fencing, set out a row of timber, concrete or angle-iron posts, spacing them no more than 3m (10ft) apart. Brace the end posts with struts to resist the pull exerted by the straining wires. A long run needs a braced intermediate post every 70m (225ft) or so.

Using timber posts

Using a turnbuckle
Apply tension by turning the turnbuckle with a metal bar.

Support chain-link fencing on straining wires. Since it's impossible to tension the heavy-gauge wire by hand, large straining bolts are used to stretch it between the posts – one to coincide with the top of the fencing, one about 150mm (6in) from the ground, and a third one midway between.

Drill 10mm (⅜in) diameter holes through the posts. Insert a bolt into each hole and fit a washer and nut (**1**), leaving enough thread to provide about 50mm (2in) movement once you begin to apply tension to the wire.

Pass the end of the wire through the eye of a bolt, then twist it around itself with pliers (**2**). Stretch the wire along the run of fencing, stapling it to each post and strut (**3**), but leave enough slack for the wire to move when tensioned.

Cut the wire to length and twist it through the bolt at the other end of the fence. Tension the wire from both ends by turning the nuts with a spanner (**4**).

Standard straining bolts provide enough tension for the average garden fence, but over a long run of fencing – 70m (225ft) or more – use a turnbuckle for each wire, applying tension with a metal bar (see left).

Attaching the mesh
Staple each end link to the post (**5**). Unroll the mesh and pull it taut. Tie it to straining wires every 300mm (1ft) with galvanized wire (**6**). Fix to the post at the far end.

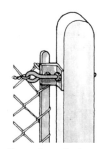

Cleat and stretcher bar

Wire tied to post

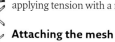

Using concrete posts

Fix straining wires to concrete posts, using a special bolt and cleat (see above left). Bolt a stretcher bar to the cleats when erecting the wire netting. Secure the straining wires to intermediate posts by using a length of galvanized wire passed through each of the predrilled holes.

Winding bracket

Using angle-iron posts

Stretcher bars with winding brackets for applying tension to straining wires are supplied with angle-iron fence posts (see left). Pass the straining wire through the hole in every intermediate post.

Wire goes through post

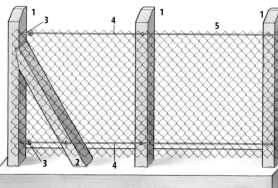

Chain-link fencing
1 Post
2 Strut
3 Straining bolt
4 Straining wire
5 Wire mesh

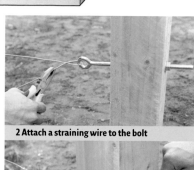

1 Insert a straining bolt in the end post

2 Attach a straining wire to the bolt

3 Staple the wire to each post and strut

4 Tension the bolt at the far end of the fence

5 Staple mesh to post

6 Tie with wire loops

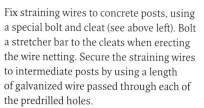

NOTCHED END POST
INTERMEDIATE POST
BOLTED CLEAT
STRETCHER BAR
STRAINING WIRES
STRUT
BOLTED CLEAT

Concrete fence posts

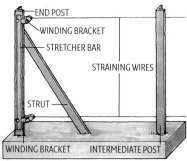

END POST
WINDING BRACKET
STRETCHER BAR
STRAINING WIRES
STRUT
WINDING BRACKET   INTERMEDIATE POST

Angle-iron posts

SEE ALSO > Fence posts 12–13, Bracing struts 13

Erecting closeboard fences

The featherboards used to panel a closeboard fence are nailed to triangular-section arris rails mortised into the fence posts. Concrete posts – and some wooden ones – are supplied ready-mortised, but if you buy standard timber posts you'll either have to cut the mortises yourself or use end brackets (see below right) instead. Space fence posts no more than 3m (10ft) apart. Fix horizontal gravel boards at the foot of the fence. Nail capping strips across the tops of the boards.

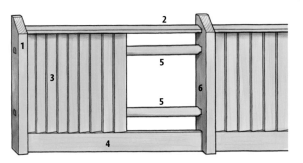

Closeboard fencing
1 End post
2 Capping strip
3 Featherboards
4 Gravel board
5 Arris rail
6 Intermediate post

Erecting the framework

When using plain wooden posts, mark and cut 50 x 22mm (2 x ⅞in) mortises for the arris rails, about 150mm (6in) above and below the ends of the fixed featherboards. For fencing more than 1.2m (4ft) high, cut mortises for a third rail midway between the others. Position the mortises 25mm (1in) from the front face of each post (the face on the featherboarded side of the fence).

As you erect the fence, cut the rails to length and shape a tenon on each end, using a coarse rasp or Surform file (**1**). Paint preserver onto the shaped ends and into the mortises before you assemble the rails.

Erect the first fence post and pack hardcore around its base. Get someone to hold the post steady while you fit the arris rails and erect the next post, tapping it onto the ends of the rails with a mallet (**2**). Check that the rails are horizontal and the posts vertical before packing hardcore around the second post. Construct the entire run of posts and rails in the same way. If you can't manoeuvre the last post onto the tenoned rails, cut the rails square and fix them to the post with metal end brackets.

Check the whole run once more to ensure that the rails are bedded firmly in their mortises and that the framework is true, then secure each rail by driving a nail through the post into the tenon (**3**) or by drilling a hole and inserting a wooden dowel. Pack concrete around each post and leave it to set.

Fitting the boards

Gravel boards

Some concrete posts are mortised to take gravel boards; fit the boards at the same time as the arris rails. If concrete posts are not mortised, bed treated wooden cleats into the concrete filling at the base of each post and screw the gravel board to the cleat when the concrete has set.

To fit gravel boards to wooden posts, skew-nail cleats to the foot of each post, then nail the boards to the cleats (**4**). Some metal post sockets are made with brackets for attaching gravel boards.

Featherboards

Cut the featherboards to length and treat the end grain with preservative. Stand the first featherboard on the gravel board, butting its thicker edge against the post. Nail the board to the arris rails with galvanized nails, about 18mm (¾in) from the thick edge. Place the next featherboard in position, overlapping the thin edge of the fixed board by 12mm (½in). Check that it's vertical, then nail it in the same way. Don't drive a nail through both boards, or they may split should the wood shrink. To space the other boards equally, make a spacer block from a scrap of wood (**5**).

Plane the last board to fit against the next post and fix it, this time with two nails per rail. Finally, nail capping strips along the tops of the featherboards, then cut the posts to length and cap them.

1 Shape the arris rails to fit the mortises

2 Tap post onto the rails

3 Nail rails in place

4 Nail gravel boards to the cleats

5 Use a spacer block to position featherboards

End brackets
Instead of cutting mortise-and-tenon joints, you can use special metal brackets to join arris rails to fence posts.

Capping the fence
Nail a wooden capping strip to the ends of the featherboards to shed rainwater.

SEE ALSO > Capping fence posts 12, Erecting fence posts 13, Fence-post sockets 13

Erecting panel fencing

To prevent a prefabricated panel rotting, either fit gravel boards – as on a closeboard fence – or leave a gap at the bottom by supporting a panel temporarily on two bricks while you fix it to the fence posts.

Using timber posts

Pack the first post into its hole with hardcore. Then get someone to hold a panel against the post while you skew-nail through the frame into the post. If you can work from both sides, drive three nails from each side of the fence. If the wood used for the frame is likely to split, blunt the nails by tapping their points with a hammer. Alternatively, use rust-proofed metal angle brackets to secure the panels. Construct the entire fence by erecting panels and posts alternately.

Fit pressure-treated gravel boards; and nail capping strips along the panels, if they have not already been fitted by the manufacturer. Finally, cut each post to length and cap it.

Wedge struts made from scrap timber against each post to keep it vertical, then top up the holes with concrete. If you're unable to work from both sides, you will have to fill each hole as you build the fence.

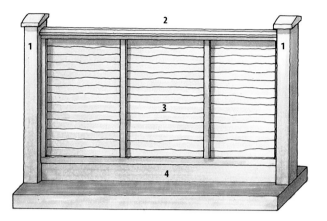

Panel fence
1 Fence posts
2 Capping strip
3 Prefabricated panel
4 Gravel board

Nail the panel through its frame

Or use angle brackets to fix panels to posts

Using concrete posts

Grooved concrete fence posts will support prefabricated panels without the need for additional fixings.

Concrete post grooved to take panels

Building a panel fence
Support a panel on bricks and get a helper to push it against the post while you nail it.

SEE ALSO > Capping fence posts 12, Erecting fence posts 13, Concrete 38–45

Post-and-rail fences

A simple ranch-style fence is no more than a series of horizontal rails fixed to short posts concreted into the ground. A picket fence is constructed similarly, but with vertical pales fixed to the rails.

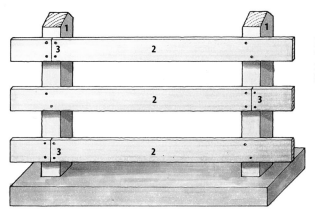

Ranch-style fence
1 Short posts
2 Horizontal rails
3 Rail joints

Erecting fences on sloping ground

Slope running across
If a slope runs across your garden so that a neighbour's garden is higher than your own, either build brick retaining walls between the posts or set paving slabs in concrete to hold back the soil.

Downhill slope
The posts need to be set vertically, even when you are erecting a fence on a sloping site. Chain-link fencing or ranch-style rails can follow the slope of the land if you wish; but fence panels should be stepped and the triangular gaps beneath them filled with gravel boards or retaining walls.

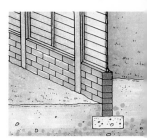

Retaining wall for a crossways slope

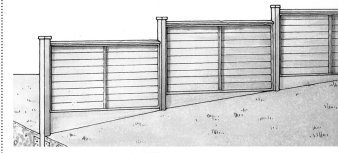

Step fence panels to allow for a downhill slope

Fixing horizontal rails

You can screw the rails directly to the posts, but the fence is likely to last longer if you cut a shallow notch in the post to locate each rail before fixing it permanently in place.

Join two horizontal rails by butting them over a fence post. Arrange to stagger such joints so that you don't end up with all the rails butted on the same posts.

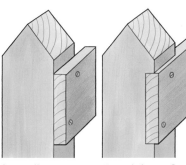

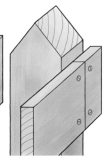

Building plastic ranch-style fencing
The basic construction of a plastic ranch-style fence is similar to one built from timber – but follow the manufacturer's instructions concerning the method for joining the rails to the posts.

Screw rail to post   **Or notch the post first**   **Butt rails on posts**

Fixing picket panels

When constructing a low picket fence from ready-made panels – which are designed to fit between the posts – it is best to either buy or make metal brackets

for attaching a pair of panels to each post. Be sure to prime and paint home-made steel brackets to prevent the metal corroding.

Use metal brackets to fix picket-fence panels

Supporting a rotted post

Buried timber posts often rot below ground level, leaving a perfectly sound section above. To save buying a whole new post, you can make a passable repair by bracing the upper section with a short concrete spur.

Erecting the spur
First, dig the soil from around the rotted stump and remove it. Insert the spur and pack hardcore around it (**1**), then fill with concrete (**2**). Drill pilot holes in the wooden post for coach screws – woodscrews with hexagonal heads (**3**). Insert the screws, using a spanner to draw the post tightly against the spur.

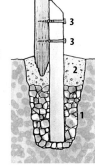

SEE ALSO > Erecting fence posts 13, Building walls 26–36

Choosing a gate

Browsing through suppliers' catalogues, you will find that gates are grouped according to their intended location – because it's where a gate is hung that has the greatest influence on its design and style. When choosing a gate, give due consideration to the character of the house and its surroundings. Buy a gate that matches the style of fence or complements the wall from which it is hung. If in doubt, aim for simplicity.

Side gates

An unprotected side entrance is an open invitation for intruders to slip in unnoticed and gain access to the back of your house. Side gates are designed to deter burglars while affording easy access for tradesmen. These gates are invariably 2m (6ft 6in) high and are made either from wrought iron or from stout sections of timber. Wooden gates are heavy and are therefore braced with strong diagonal members to keep them rigid. With security in mind, choose a closeboarded or tongued and grooved gate – as their vertical boards are difficult to climb. Fit strong bolts top and bottom.

Entrance gates

An entrance gate is designed as much for its appearance as its function, but it must be sturdy enough to withstand frequent use. For this reason, wooden gates are often braced with a diagonal strut running from the top of the latch stile down to the bottom of the hanging or hinge stile. Don't hang a gate with the strut running the other way, or the bracing will have no effect whatsoever.

Common fence styles are reflected in the type of entrance gates you can buy. Picket, closeboard and ranch-style gates are all available, and there are simple frame-and-panel gates made with solid timber or exterior-grade plywood panels that serve to keep the frame rigid. If the tops of both the stiles (uprights) are cut at an angle, they will tend to shed rainwater, reducing the likelihood of wet rot.

Decorative iron gates are often used for entrances, but make sure the style is appropriate for the building and its location. An ostentatious gate may look out of place in front of a simple modern house or a country cottage.

Drive gates

First, decide whether hanging a gate across your drive is a good idea. Stepping out of your car into the road in order to open the gate can be dangerous unless there's plenty of room to park the vehicle temporarily in front of the gate.

Drive gates invariably open into the property; so if the drive slopes up from the road, make sure there's adequate ground clearance for a wide gate. Alternatively, hang a pair of smaller gates that meet in the centre.

Gateposts and piers

Gateposts and masonry piers need to be anchored securely to the ground, to take the leverage exerted by a heavy gate. This is especially important for relatively wide drive gates.

Choose hardwood posts whenever possible, and select the size according to the weight of the gate. Posts 100mm (4in) square are adequate for entrance gates, but use 125mm (5in) posts for gates that are 2m (6ft 6in) high. For a gate across a drive, choose posts 150mm (6in) or even 200mm (8in) square.

If you opt for concrete gateposts, look for posts predrilled to accept hinges and a catch. Otherwise, you'll have to screw these fittings to a strip of timber bolted securely to the post.

Square or cylindrical tubular-steel posts are available with hinge pins, gatestops and catches welded in place. Unless they are plastic-coated, metal posts need to be painted to protect them from rust.

A pair of masonry piers is another possibility. Each pier should be at least 328mm (1ft 1½in) square and built on a firm concrete footing. For heavy gates, the hinge pier should be reinforced with a metal rod buried in the footing and running centrally through the pier.

SEE ALSO > Footings 27, Building piers 32–3

Hardware for gates

A range of specialized hardware has been developed for hanging heavy garden gates, to cope with the strain on their fixings.

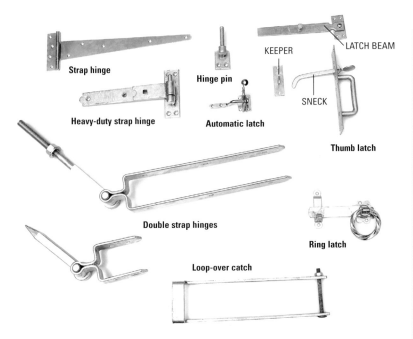

Strap hinge

Hinge pin

KEEPER

LATCH BEAM

SNECK

Heavy-duty strap hinge

Automatic latch

Thumb latch

Double strap hinges

Ring latch

Loop-over catch

Hinges

Strap hinges

Most side and entrance gates are hung on strap hinges. Screw the longer flap to the gate rail, and the vertical flap to the face of the post. Heavy gates require a hinge that's bolted through the top rail.

Wide drive gates are best hung from double strap hinges, made with long flaps bolted on each side of the top rail.

Hinge pins

Collars welded to metal gates drop over hinge pins attached to the gateposts. To prevent a gate being lifted off its hinges, drill a hole through the top pin and fit a split pin and washer.

Latches and catches

Automatic latches

Simple wooden gates are usually fitted with a latch that operates automatically as the gate is closed.

Thumb latches

Pass the sneck (lifter bar) of a thumb latch through a slot cut in the gate, then screw the handle to the front. Screw the latch beam to the inner face, where the sneck can lift the beam from the hooked keeper fixed to the gatepost.

Ring latches

A ring latch works in a similar way to a thumb latch but is usually operated, from inside only, by twisting the ring handle to lift the latch beam.

Loop-over catches

When hanging a pair of wide gates, one is fixed with a bolt that locates in a socket concreted into the ground. A U-shape metal catch on the other gate drops over the stile of the fixed gate.

Materials for gates

Although wooden gates are often made from relatively cheap softwood, a wood such as cedar or oak will last longer. Most so-called 'wrought-iron' gates are made from mild-steel bar, which must be primed and painted.

Gateposts

Gateposts are set in concrete, but the post holes should be linked by a concrete bridge to provide extra support.

Erecting gateposts

Lay the gate on the ground with a post on each side. Check that the posts are parallel and that they are the required distance apart to accommodate hinges and catch. Nail two battens from post to post and another diagonally to keep the posts in line while you erect them (**1**).

Dig a trench across the entrance, making it 300mm (1ft) wide and long enough to take both posts. It need be no deeper than 300mm (1ft) in the centre, but dig a post hole at each end – 450mm (1ft 6in) deep for a low entrance gate, 600mm (2ft) deep for a tall side gate.

Set the battened gateposts in the holes with hardcore and concrete, using temporary battens to hold them upright until the concrete has set (**2**).

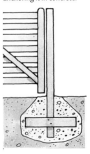

Drive gateposts
Hang wide farm-style gates on posts set in holes 900mm (3ft) deep. Erect the latch post in concrete, like any fence post, but bolt a stout piece of timber across the base of the hinge post before anchoring it in concrete.

Supporting wide gates
Bolt a balk of timber to the hinge post to help support the weight of a wide gate.

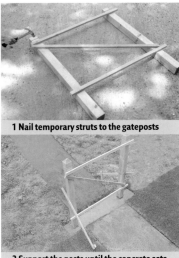

1 Nail temporary struts to the gateposts

2 Support the posts until the concrete sets

Hanging a gate
Stand the gate between the posts and prop it up on a pair or bricks or wooden blocks to hold it at the required height off the ground. Tap in pairs of wedges on each side of the gate until it is held securely. Then mark the positions of the hinges and catch.

SEE ALSO > Erecting fence posts 13

Building walls

Whatever kind of masonry structure you are building, the basic techniques are broadly similar. However, it's well worth hiring a professional builder or bricklayer when the structure is complicated or extensive, especially if it will have to bear considerable loads or stress.

Walls for different locations

Compressive strength of bricks
The compressive strength of bricks is specified in Newtons per square millimetre (N/mm²). Average-strength facings will generally be rated about 20N/mm². Class A engineering bricks have a compressive strength of not less than 70N/mm², Class B a strength of not less than 50N/mm².

Retaining walls

A retaining wall is designed to hold back a bank of earth when terracing a sloping site. Raised planting beds often serve a similar purpose.

Provided it's not excessively high, a retaining wall is quite easy to build, although strictly speaking it should slope back into the bank to resist the weight of the earth. You must also allow for drainage, in order to reduce water pressure behind the wall.

Retaining walls can be constructed with bricks, concrete blocks or stone. Sometimes they are dry-laid, with earth packed into the crevices between stones in order to accommodate plants.

Boundary walls

A brick or stone wall that surrounds your property provides security and privacy while creating an attractive background for trees and shrubs.

New bricks complement a formal garden or a modern setting, while secondhand materials or undressed stone blend well with an old, established garden. If you aren't able to match existing masonry exactly, disguise the difference in colour by brushing liquid fertilizer onto the wall to encourage lichen to grow. Alternatively, hide the junction with a climbing plant. You need local-authority approval to build a wall higher than 1m (3ft 3in) if it adjoins a highway, or one that is over 2m (6ft 6in) high elsewhere.

Dividing walls

Many gardeners like to divide up a plot with walls in order to add interest to an otherwise featureless site. For example, you can build a wall to form a visual break between a patio and an area of grass, or perhaps to define the edge of a pathway. This type of dividing wall is often no more than 600 to 750mm (2ft to 2ft 6in) high.

Use simple concrete-block or brick walls to create separate areas inside a workshop or garage.

Screen walls

Screens are dividing walls that provide a degree of privacy without completely masking the garden beyond. They are usually built with decorative pierced blocks, sometimes combined with brick or solid-block bases and piers.

Amateur bricklayers

It is difficult to suggest which aspects of bricklaying are likely to overstretch the capabilities of an amateur builder, as this differs from one individual to another and also depends on the nature of the job. Clearly, it would be foolhardy for anyone to try to build a two-storey house without having had a great deal of experience, augmented by professional tuition. And even building a high boundary wall, which is simple in terms of technique, may be arduous if the wall is a very long one or if you have to allow for changes in gradient.

The simple answer is to practise with relatively low retaining walls, decorative screens or dividing walls until you have mastered the skills of laying bricks and concrete blocks solidly one upon another, and have developed the ability to build a wall that is straight and absolutely vertical. At that point, you may wish to move on to more demanding bricklaying projects.

Stone-built retaining wall

Decorative pierced-block screen

Boundary wall of yellow brick

Artificial-stone blocks make attractive dividing walls

SEE ALSO > Choosing bricks 21, Choosing concrete blocks 23, Mortar for building walls 25, Bonding brickwork 26, Laying bricks 28

Choosing bricks

At one time, bricks were named after their district of origin, where a particular clay imparted a distinctive colour. Nowadays names are often chosen by manufacturers to suggest the continuation of that tradition. Typical examples are London stocks, Leicester reds, Blue Staffs and so on. The colour and texture are of interest when trying to match existing masonry, but of equal importance are the variety, durability and type of brick.

Types of brick

Solid bricks
The majority of bricks are solid throughout and are either flat on all surfaces or have a depression known as a 'frog' on one face. When filled with mortar, the frog keys the bricks.

Cored or perforated bricks
Cored bricks have holes through them, performing the same function as the frog. A wall made with cored bricks must be finished with a solid-brick or slab coping.

Special shapes
Specially shaped bricks are made for decorative brickwork. Master bricklayers draw upon the full range when building structures such as arches and chamfered or rounded corners. Shaped bricks are made for coping walls.

Double-cant coping

Standard cored brick   **Bullnose brick**

Standard brick with frog   **Squint for shaped corner**   **Half-round coping**

Varieties of brick

Facings
Facings are made as much for their appearance as their structural qualities and, as such, are available in a wide range of colours and textures. Facings are used for exposed brickwork.

Commons
Commons are cheap general-purpose bricks used primarily for plastered or rendered brickwork, the inner leaf of cavity walls and foundations. They are not colour-matched as carefully as facings, but the mottled effect of a wall built with commons is not unattractive. Concrete building blocks have now all but replaced commons for cavity walling and internal partition walls.

Engineering bricks
Engineering bricks are exceptionally dense and strong. You are unlikely to need them for the average wall, but because they are impervious to water they are sometimes used to construct damp-proof courses.

Durability of bricks

Frost resistance
Freezing causes moisture within a brick to expand, which sometimes causes the surface of the brick to spall (flake). Bricks are made with different degrees of frost resistance.

   F2-category bricks are totally frost-resistant, even when a saturated wall is exposed to freezing. They are especially suitable for walls in coastal regions. These bricks were previously designated as 'special quality'.

   F1-category bricks (previously known as 'ordinary quality') are moderately frost-resistant. Though suitable for most external uses, these bricks may suffer if they are subjected to extreme weathering or if used for a retaining wall that holds back poorly drained soil.

F0-category bricks (previously designated as 'internal quality') are likely to be damaged by frost and should be used for building internal walls only. Make sure these bricks are stored under cover.

Soluble-salt content
The materials from which bricks are manufactured contain impurities, such as soluble salts, that can attack cement mortar and cause efflorescence to form on the surface of a wall.

   For general-purpose brickwork, use S1-category bricks. S0-category bricks should be used in completely dry locations only. Bricks designated S2 are intended for use in locations subjected to prolonged saturation – such as foundations and retaining walls.

• **Storing bricks**
When your bricks are delivered, stack them carefully on a flat, dry base and cover them with polythene sheet or a tarpaulin. This prevents them becoming saturated, which could cause staining as well as an increased risk of frost damage to the mortar and the bricks themselves.

Seconds
The term 'seconds' denotes second-hand, rather than second-rate, bricks. They should be cheaper than new bricks, but demand can inflate prices. Using seconds might be the only way you can match the colour of weathered brickwork.

Buying bricks

The dimensions of a standard brick are 215 x 102.5 x 65mm (8½ x 4 x 2½ in), but these sometimes vary by a few millimetres – even within the same batch of bricks. Brick manufacturers normally specify a nominal size, which includes an additional 10mm (⅜in) on each of the dimensions in order to allow for the mortar joint.

   To calculate how many bricks you will need, allow approximately 60 bricks for every square metre (50 bricks per square yard) of single-skin walling. Add an extra 5 per cent for cutting and breakages. Bricks are normally cheaper if you order them in sufficient quantity direct from the manufacturer.

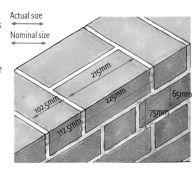

Actual size
Nominal size

215mm
102.5mm
225mm
112.5mm
75mm
65mm

SEE ALSO > Coloured and textured bricks 22, Laying bricks 28–33, Coping a wall 30

Brick colour and texture

The popularity of brick as a building material is derived largely from its range of subtle colours and textures, which actually improve with weathering. Weathered brick can be difficult to match by using a manufacturer's catalogue, so try to borrow samples from your supplier's stock – or if you have spare bricks, take one to the supplier to compare it with new bricks.

Colour

The colour of bricks is largely determined by the type of clay used for their manufacture, although their colour may be modified by the addition of certain minerals and by the temperature of firing. Large manufacturers supply a wide variety of colours; and you can also buy brindled (multicoloured or mottled) bricks, which are useful for blending with existing masonry.

Texture

Texture is as important to the appearance of a brick wall as colour. Simple rough or smooth textures are created by the choice of materials. Others are imposed upon the clay by scratching, rolling, brushing, and so on. A brick may be textured all over, or on the sides and ends only.

Decorative combination of coloured bricks

Brick colours and textures
A small selection from the wide range of colours and textures available.
1 Smooth blended
2 Handmade
3 Sandfaced yellow
4 Smooth blue engineering
5 Sandfaced grey
6 Smooth red stock
7 Wirecut brindle
8 Textured buff multi
9 London stock (second)
10 Wirecut blue
11 Red common
12 Coarse fletton
13 Moulded fletton
14 Dragfaced red multi

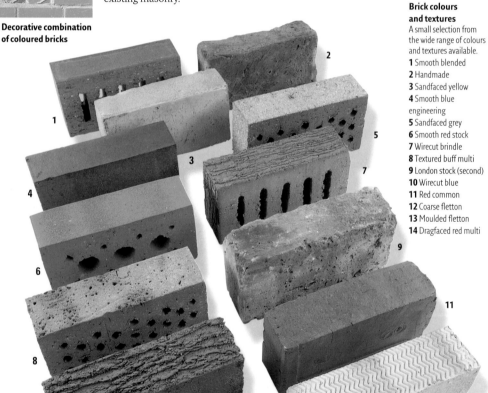

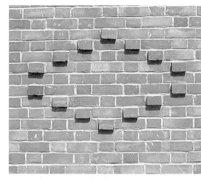

Pattern formed by projecting headers

Look out for second-hand moulded bricks

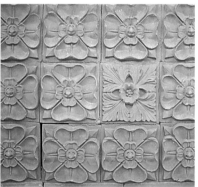

Sometimes whole panels are available

Weathered antique bricks are much sought after

SEE ALSO > Choosing bricks 21, Laying bricks 28–33

Choosing concrete blocks

Cast-concrete blocks were introduced as a cheap substitute for bricks that were to be covered with plaster or render, but they are now used in a variety of situations – from foundations to soundproof internal partitions. Indeed, modern concrete blocks are superior to clay bricks in terms of acoustic and thermal insulation.

Density

Lightweight-concrete blocks
Made from aerated or foamed concrete, these blocks can be carried easily in one hand, which enables bricklayers to build walls quickly and safely. Aerated blocks can be drilled, cut to shape and chased for electric cables, using handtools or power tools. They are used extensively in the building trade for the construction of both internal and external walls.

Dense-concrete blocks
Made from relatively heavy concrete, these are also known as dense-aggregate blocks or medium-density blocks.

Nowadays, because of the availability of lightweight loadbearing blocks, dense-concrete blocks are used less frequently, even though they are slightly cheaper than equivalent building blocks made of aerated concrete.

Varieties of block

Construction
The majority of building blocks are simple rectangular blocks of cement-grey or white concrete. The larger ones, especially if they are made from dense concrete, are available in the form of hollow blocks with enclosed supporting ribs between the outer skins. Including voids not only reduces the weight of the blocks, but allows for metal rods to be inserted in order to reinforce retaining walls. With cellular blocks, the voids are open at the bottom only.

Grades
Standard-grade blocks have no aesthetic qualities whatsoever. They are used for the structural core of a wall that is going to be either rendered or plastered, and so are usually made with zigzag 'keying' on both faces.

Fair-face building blocks, which are intended to be visible, usually have smooth faces. However, some fair-face blocks are shot-blasted in order to create a hard-wearing finely textured surface finish.

Paint-quality concrete blocks are ideal for a wall that is to be decorated directly with masonry paint.

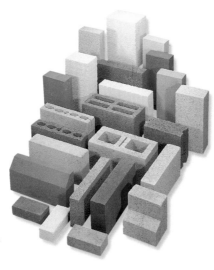

Qualities

Loadbearing
Lightweight and dense-concrete blocks are produced for non-loadbearing and load-bearing applications, but dense-concrete blocks are made in a greater range of high compressive strengths. Even so, it's possible to buy lightweight blocks that are perfectly suited to building loadbearing foundations and multistorey dwellings.

Insulating
Aerated blocks greatly reduce the trans-mission of heat and sound. Blocks with superior acoustic-insulation properties are made specifically for partitions and party walls. Those that have a high degree of thermal insulation reduce the need for secondary insulation.

Moisture and frost resistance
Most concrete blocks are generally weatherproof. Totally frost-resistant and moisture-proof blocks are made for foundations and walling below ground.

Buying blocks

When the blocks are delivered, have them unloaded as near as possible to the construction site. Stack them on a flat, dry base and protect them from rain and frost with a polythene sheet.

Available sizes
The average concrete block measures 450 x 225mm (1ft 6in x 9in) and ranges in thickness from 75 to 230mm (3 to 9in). Specials – such as foundation blocks – may be similar in length and height but may differ in thickness. Brick-size concrete blocks, known as coursing bricks, are made for infilling above door and window lintels.

The dimensions given above are actual sizes, but some manufacturers may specify nominal sizes (also known as 'coordinating sizes'), which include a 10mm (⅜in) allowance for mortar on the length and height. Since block walls are often constructed with just one skin of masonry, the thickness of a block is normally given as the actual size.

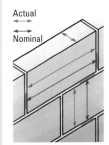

Sizes of structural blocks
The nominal size of a block refers to the length and height only. The thickness is always specified as the actual size.

Screen blocks

Pierced concrete blocks are used for building decorative screens in the garden. The blocks are not bonded like brickwork or structural blocks and therefore require supporting brick piers. Matching coping slabs and pier caps are available for finishing the top of the screen.

Screen blocks should not be used to build loadbearing walls, but they can support a lightweight structure.

Standard sizes
Decorative screen blocks are invariably 300mm (1ft) square and 90mm (about 3½in) thick.

SEE ALSO > Compressive strength 20, Laying bricks 28–33, Coping a wall 30

Stone: natural and artificial

Artificial-stone blocks, made from poured concrete, can look very convincing once they have weathered. Depending on where you live, these blocks may be easier to obtain than natural building stone, and are probably cheaper. Aesthetically, however, nothing can surpass quarried stone, such as granite or sandstone.

Natural stone

Limestone, sandstone and granite are all suitable materials for building walls. Flint and slate are laid using specialized methods, and both are frequently used in combination with other materials.

Stone bought in its natural state is classed as random rubble (undressed); it is a perfect choice for dry-stone walling in an informal garden setting. For more regular masonry, ask for squared rubble (semi-dressed) stone, which is cut into reasonably uniform blocks but with uneven surfaces. Ashlar is fully dressed stone with machine-cut faces. The cost of stone increases in proportion to the degree of preparation required.

Natural stone
Whether it be roughly hewn or finely dressed, natural stone is durable and weathers superbly.

Artificial-stone walling
(below left)
Cast-concrete blocks that simulate real stonework are used to construct attractive walling and planters.

Slate-effect walling
(below right)
Good-quality concrete walling is difficult to distinguish from real slate once it has weathered. What looks like narrow sections of slate are actually cast as large interlocking blocks that can be laid quickly.

Semi-dressed natural-stone blocks

Dry-stone retaining wall

Split-stone walling

Knapped-flint boundary wall

Obtaining stone

In practical terms, the type of stone you can use for walling depends almost entirely on where you live. In some parts of the country there are restrictions governing the choice of building materials – and, in any case, a structure built from indigenous stone is more likely to blend into its surroundings. Buying stone from a local quarry also makes economical sense. Most quarries sell stone by the tonne, and will be able to give you advice on quantity and price.

If you live in a town or city, obtaining natural stone can be a problem. You may be prepared to buy a few small boulders for a rockery from a local garden centre, but the cost of buying enough stone for even a short run of walling is likely to be prohibitive. If you don't want to use artificial stone made from cast concrete, your only alternative is to hire a truck and drive to a quarry out of town.

Another source of materials, and possibly the cheapest way to obtain dressed stone, is to visit a demolition site. Prices vary considerably, but the cost of transport may be less than a trip to a quarry.

Artificial-stone blocks

The stretcher faces of concrete blocks made specifically for garden walling are textured to resemble natural stone. Single blocks are laid in mortar and bonded like real stonework; and there are larger blocks that look like two or three courses of squared rubble or dressed stone.

SEE ALSO > Choosing concrete blocks 23, Laying blocks 34, Building with stone 35, Building retaining walls 36

Mortar for building walls

Mortar is employed to bind together bricks, concrete blocks or stones. The durability of the wall depends to a certain extent upon the quality of the mortar used in its construction. If it's mixed correctly, mortar is strong yet flexible – but if the ingredients are in the wrong proportions, the mortar is likely to be weak or, conversely, so hard that it is prone to cracking. If too much water is added to the mix, the mortar will be squeezed out of the joints by the weight of the masonry. If the mortar is too dry, then adhesion will be poor.

Correct consistency
The mortar mix should be firm enough to hold its shape when you make a depression in the mix.

● **Lime mortar**
Much old brickwork was built using lime mortar. When cement-based mortar is used to repoint soft brickwork there's an increased risk of spalling and cracked pointing. You can buy powdered hydraulic lime to mix with sand and water: 1 part lime to 2.5 parts sand. Mix to the consistency of cottage cheese. Wear gloves and goggles when handling lime.

The ingredients of mortar

General-purpose mortar is made from cement, hydrated lime and sand, mixed together with enough water to make a workable paste.

Cement is the hardening agent that binds the other ingredients together. The lime slows down the drying process and prevents the mortar setting too quickly. It also makes the mix flow well, so that it fills gaps in the masonry and adheres to the texture of blocks or bricks. Sand acts as an aggregate, adding body to the mortar, and reduces the possibility of shrinkage.

For general-purpose mortar, fine builder's sand is ideal – but if you want a pale mortar for bonding white screen blocks, use silver sand instead.

Plasticizers

If you're laying masonry in a period of cold weather, substitute a proprietary plasticizer for the lime. The plasticizer produces an aerated mortar in which the tiny air bubbles allow water to expand in freezing conditions, thus reducing the risk of cracking. Premixed masonry cement, which has an aerating agent, is ready for mixing with sand.

Ready-mixed mortar

This type of mortar contains all the essential ingredients mixed to the correct proportions – you simply add water.

Mixing mortar

Mortar should be discarded if it isn't used within 2 hours of being mixed – so make only as much as you can use within that time. An average of about 2 minutes for laying each brick is a reasonable estimate.

Choose a flat site upon which to mix the materials – a sheet of plywood will do – and dampen it slightly, in order to prevent it absorbing water from the mortar. Make a pile of half the amount of sand that is to be used, then add the other ingredients. Put the rest of the sand on top, and mix the dry materials thoroughly.

Scoop a depression in the pile and add clean tap water – never use contaminated or salty water. Push the dry mix from around the edge of the pile into the water until it has absorbed enough for you to blend the mix with a shovel, using a chopping action. Add more water, little by little, until the mortar has a butter-like consistency – slipping easily from the shovel, but firm enough to hold its shape if you make a hollow in the mix. If the sides of the hollow collapse, add more dry ingredients until the mortar firms up. Make sure the mortar is sufficiently moist – since dry mortar won't form a strong bond with the masonry. If the mortar stiffens up while you are working, add just enough water to restore the consistency.

Proportions for masonry mixes

Mix the ingredients according to the prevailing conditions at the building site. Use a general-purpose mortar for moderate conditions where the wall is reasonably sheltered. A stronger mix is required for severe conditions where the wall will be exposed to wind and driving rain, or if the site is elevated or near the coast. If you're using plasticizer rather than lime, follow the manufacturer's instructions regarding the quantity you should add to the sand.

● **Estimating quantity**
When building a single-skin wall, allow approximately 1cu m (1⅓ cu yd) of sand (other ingredients in proportion) to lay either 3364 bricks, 1946 average concrete blocks, or 1639 decorative screen blocks.

Masonry cement
This is a ready-mixed cement that's used without adding lime or plasticizer.

MORTAR-MIXING PROPORTIONS		
Cement/lime mortar	Plasticized mortar	Masonry cement
General-purpose mortar (moderate conditions)		
1 part cement 1 part lime 6 parts sand	1 part cement 6 parts sand/plasticizer	1 part masonry cement 5 parts sand
Strong mortar (severe conditions)		
1 part cement ½ part lime 4 parts sand	1 part cement 4 parts sand/plasticizer	1 part masonry cement 3 parts sand

Bricklayers' terms

Bricklayers use a number of specialized terms to describe their craft and materials. Those used frequently are listed below, others are described as they occur.

BRICK FACES (the surfaces of a brick)
Stretcher faces – the long sides of a brick
Header faces – the short ends of a brick
Bedding faces – the top and bottom surfaces
Frog – the depression in one bedding face

COURSE (horizontal row of bricks)
Stretcher course – a single course with stretcher faces visible
Header course – a single course with header faces visible
Coping – the top course designed to protect the wall from rainwater
Bond – the pattern produced by staggering alternate courses so that vertical joints are not aligned one above the other
Stretcher – a single brick from a stretcher course
Header – a single brick from a header course
Closure brick – the last brick laid in a course

CUT BRICKS (bricks cut to even up the bond)
Bat – a brick cut across its width (e.g. half bat, three-quarter bat)
Queen closer – a brick cut along its length

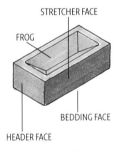

STRETCHER FACE

FROG

BEDDING FACE

HEADER FACE

HALF BAT

QUEEN CLOSER

SEE ALSO ▶ Cutting bricks 28

Bonding brickwork

Although mortar is extremely strong under compression, its tensile strength is relatively weak. If bricks were stacked one upon the other, so that the vertical joints were continuous, any movement within the wall would pull the joints apart. Bonding the brickwork staggers the vertical joints, transmitting the load along the entire length of the wall.

Stretcher bond

Stretcher bond

The stretcher bond is used for single-thickness walls – including the two leaves of a cavity wall employed in the construction of modern buildings. Half bats are used to complete the bond at the end of a straight wall, while a corner is formed by alternating headers and stretchers.

English bond

If you were to build a wall 215mm (8½in) thick by laying courses of stretcher-bonded bricks side by side, there would be a weak vertical joint running centrally down the wall. An English bond strengthens the wall by using alternate courses of headers. Staggered joints are maintained at the end of the wall and at right-angle corners by inserting a queen closer before the last header.

Flemish bond

Flemish bond

The Flemish bond is another method used for building a solid wall 215mm (8½in) thick. Every course is laid with alternate headers and stretchers. Stagger the joint at the end of a course and at corners by laying a queen closer before the header.

Decorative bonds

Stretcher, English and Flemish bonds are designed to construct strong walls; decorative qualities are incidental. Other bonds, used primarily for their visual effect, are suitable for low non-loadbearing walls only. They need to be supported by a conventionally bonded base and piers.

Honeycomb bond

Stack bonding

Laying bricks in groups of three creates a basket-weave effect. Strengthen the continuous vertical joints with wall ties.

Honeycomb bond

You can build an open decorative screen by using a stretcher-like bond with a quarter-bat-size space between each brick. This type of screen has to be built with care, in order to keep the bond regular. Cut quarter bats to fill the gaps in the top course.

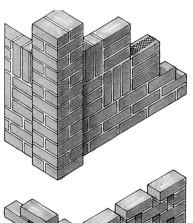

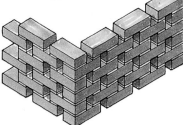

Strength and stability

It is easy enough to appreciate the loads and stresses imposed upon the walls of a house or outbuilding – and hence the need for solid foundations with adequate methods of reinforcement and protection to prevent them collapsing. But it is not so obvious that even simple garden walling requires similar measures to ensure its stability. It's merely irritating if a low dividing wall or planter falls apart, but a serious injury could result from the collapse of a heavy boundary wall.

The basic structure of a wall

Unless you design and build a wall in the correct manner, it will not be strong and stable.

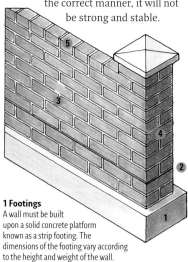

1 Footings
A wall must be built upon a solid concrete platform known as a strip footing. The dimensions of the footing vary according to the height and weight of the wall.

2 Damp-proof course
A layer of waterproof material 150mm (6in) above ground level stops water rising from the soil. It is not required for most garden walling unless the wall abuts a building with a similar DPC.

3 Bonding
The staggered pattern of the bricks is not merely decorative. It's designed primarily to spread the static load along the wall and to tie the individual bricks together.

4 Piers
Straight walls that exceed a certain height and length must be buttressed at regular intervals with thick columns of brickwork, known as piers.

5 Coping
The coping prevents frost damage by shedding rainwater, which could seep into the upper brick joints.

SEE ALSO > Choosing bricks 21–2, Copings 30, Wall ties 32, Building piers 32–3

Footings for garden walls

The Building Regulations govern the size and reinforcement of the footings required to support high walls, especially loadbearing walls. However, the majority of garden walls can be built upon concrete footings laid in a straight-sided trench.

Size of footings

The footing needs to be sufficiently substantial to support the weight of the wall. The surrounding soil must be firm and well drained, to avoid possible subsidence. It is unwise to set footings in ground that has been infilled recently, such as a new building site. Take care also to avoid tree roots and drainpipes. If the trench begins to fill with water as you are digging, seek professional advice before proceeding.

Dig the trench deeper than the footing itself, so that the first one or two courses of brick are below ground level. This will allow for an adequate depth of soil for planting right up to the wall.

If the soil is not firmly packed when you reach the required depth, dig deeper until you reach a firm level; then fill the bottom of the trench with compacted hardcore up to the lowest level of the proposed footing.

Sloping sites

If the ground slopes gently, simply ignore the gradient and make footings perfectly level. If the site slopes noticeably, make a stepped footing by placing plywood shuttering across the trench at regular intervals. Calculate the height and length of the steps, using multiples of normal brick size.

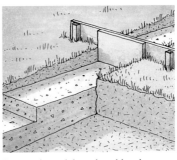

Support plywood shuttering with stakes

RECOMMENDED DIMENSIONS FOR FOOTINGS			
Type of wall	**Height of wall**	**Thickness of footing**	**Width of footing**
One brick thick	Up to 1m (3ft 3in)	150mm (6in)	300mm (1ft)
Two bricks thick	Up to 1m (3ft 3in)	225 to 300mm (9in to 1ft)	450mm (1ft 6in)
Two bricks thick	Over 1m (3ft 3in) up to 2m (6ft 6in)	375 to 450mm (1ft 3in to 1ft 6in)	450 to 600mm (1ft 6in to 2ft)
Retaining wall	Up to 1m (3ft 3in)	150 to 300mm (6in to 1ft)	375 to 450mm (1ft 3in to 1ft 6in)

Setting out the footings

For a straight footing, set up two profile boards (see right) made from timber 25mm (1in) thick nailed to stakes that are driven into the ground at each end of the proposed trench, but well outside the work area.

Drive nails into the top edge of each board and stretch lines between them to mark the front and back edges of the wall. Then drive nails into the boards on each side of the wall line to indicate the width of the footing, and stretch other lines between these nails (**1**). Next, remove the lines marking the wall – but leave the nails in place, so that you can replace the lines when you lay the bricks.

Place a spirit level against the remaining lines to mark the edge of the footing on the ground (**2**). Mark the ends of the footing, which should extend beyond the end of the wall by half the wall's thickness. Before you remove the lines, mark out each edge of the trench on the ground, using a spade. Leave the profile boards in place.

Turning corners

If your wall is going to have a right-angled corner, set up two sets of profile boards. Check carefully that the lines form a true right angle, using the 3 : 4 : 5 principle (**3**).

Profile board

Digging the trench

Excavate the trench, keeping the sides vertical; and check that the bottom is level, using a long straight piece of wood and a spirit level. Drive a stake into the bottom of the trench, near one end, until the top of the stake represents the depth of the footing. Drive in more stakes at about 1m (3ft) intervals and check that the tops are level (**4**).

Filling the trench

Pour a foundation mix of concrete (see MIXING CONCRETE BY VOLUME) into the trench, then tamp it down firmly with a stout piece of timber until it is exactly level with the top of the stakes. Leave the stakes in place, and allow the footing to harden thoroughly before building the wall.

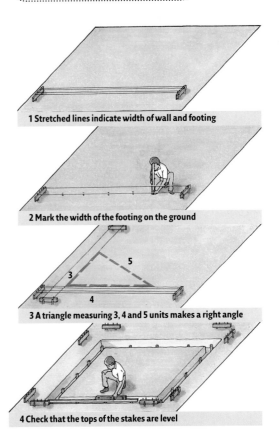

1 Stretched lines indicate width of wall and footing

2 Mark the width of the footing on the ground

3 A triangle measuring 3, 4 and 5 units makes a right angle

4 Check that the tops of the stakes are level

SEE ALSO > Mixing concrete 39–41

Laying bricks

Spreading a bed of mortar ('throwing a line') requires practice before you can do it at speed – so at first concentrate on laying bricks accurately. Using mortar of exactly the right consistency helps to keep the visible faces of the bricks clean. In hot, dry weather dampen the footings and bricks before you begin, but let any surface water evaporate before you lay the bricks.

Tools for basic bricklaying
Although you can improvise a number of builder's tools, you will have to buy some of the more specialized tools that are used by bricklayers.

● **Brick cleaner**
Wash mortar off your tools as soon as the job is finished. If need be, use an acidic brick cleaner to remove hardened mortar. Follow manufacturers' instructions carefully, and wear PVC gloves and goggles.

Spirit level

Club hammer

Bolster chisel

Pointing trowel

Brick trowel

Basic bricklaying techniques

Hold the trowel with your thumb in line with the handle and pointing towards the tip of the blade (**1**).

Scoop a measure of mortar out of the pile and shape it roughly to match the dimensions of the trowel blade. Pick up the mortar by sliding the blade under the pile, settling the mortar onto the trowel with a slight jerk of the wrist (**2**).

Spread the mortar along the top course by aligning the edge of the trowel with the centre line of the bricks (**3**). As you tip the blade to deposit the mortar, draw the trowel back towards you to stretch the bed over two to three bricks. Furrow the mortar by pressing the point of the trowel along the centre of the bed (**4**).

Pick up a brick with your other hand (**5**), but don't extend your thumb too far onto the stretcher face or it will disturb the bricklayer's line (see opposite) as you place the brick in position. Press the brick into the bed, picking up excess mortar squeezed from the joint by sliding the edge of the trowel along the face of the wall (**6**).

Spread mortar onto the header of the next brick, making a neat 10mm (³⁄₈in) bed for the header joint (**7**). Press the brick against its neighbour, scooping off excess mortar with the trowel.

Having laid three bricks, use a spirit level to check that they are horizontal. Make any adjustments by tapping them down with the trowel handle (**8**).

Hold the spirit level along the outer edge of the bricks to check that they are in line. To move a brick sideways, tap the upper edge with the trowel at about 45 degrees (**9**).

Cutting bricks
To cut bricks, use a bolster chisel to mark the line on all faces by tapping gently with a hammer. Realign the blade on the visible stretcher face and strike the chisel firmly.

1 The correct way to hold a brick trowel

2 Scoop a measure of mortar onto the trowel

3 Stretch the bed of mortar along the course

4 Furrow the mortar with the point of the trowel

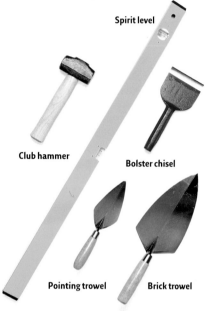
5 Pick up a brick with your thumb on the edge

6 Push the brick down and remove excess mortar

7 Spread mortar onto the head of the next brick

8 Level the bricks with the trowel handle

9 Tap the bricks sideways to align them

SEE ALSO > Choosing bricks 21–2, Mixing mortar 25, Building tools 64–7

Building a stretcher-bonded wall

Over a certain height, a single-width brick wall is structurally weak unless it is either supported with piers or changes direction by forming right-angle corners. The ability to construct accurate right-angle corners is a requirement for building most structures, even simple garden planters.

Setting out the corners

Mark out the footings and the face of the wall by stretching string lines between profile boards (see SETTING OUT THE FOOTINGS).

When the footings have been filled and the concrete has set, either use a plumb line or hold a spirit level lightly against the lines to mark the corners and the face of the wall on the footing (**1**). Join up the marks on the concrete, using a pencil and a straight batten, then check the accuracy of the corners with a builder's square.

Finally, check that the alignment is straight by stretching a string line between the corner marks.

1 Mark the face of the wall on the footing

Building corners

Construct the corners first as a series of steps or 'leads'. Throw a bed of mortar on the footing, and then lay three bricks in both directions against the marked line. Using a spirit level, make sure the bricks are level in all directions, including across the diagonal (**2**).

Build the leads to a height of five stepped courses, using a marked-out gauge stick to measure the height of each course as you proceed (**3**). Use alternate headers and stretchers to form the actual point of the corner.

Plumb the corner, and check the alignment of the stepped bricks by holding a spirit level against them (**4**).

2 Level the first course of bricks

3 Check the height with a gauge stick

4 Check that the steps are in line

• **Protecting a wall**
To protect the brickwork from rain or frost, cover newly built walls overnight with sheets of polythene or a tarpaulin. Weight the edges of the covers with bricks.

Bricklayer's line
Bricklayers use a nylon line as a guide for keeping bricks level. The line is stretched between two flat-bladed pins that are driven into vertical joints at each end of the wall.

Building the straight sections

Stretch a bricklayer's line between the corners so that it aligns perfectly with the top of the first course (**5**).

Lay the first straight course of bricks from both ends towards the middle. As you near the middle point, lay the last few bricks dry to make certain they will fit. If necessary, cut the central or 'closure' brick to fit. Mortar the bricks in place, and finish by spreading mortar onto both ends of the closure brick and onto the header faces of the bricks on each side (**6**). Scoop off excess mortar with the trowel. Lay subsequent courses between the leads in the same way, raising the bricklayer's line each time.

To build the wall higher, raise the corners first, by constructing leads to the required height, and then fill in between with bricks.

5 Stretch a bricklayer's line for the first course

6 Lay the last, or 'closure', brick carefully

SEE ALSO > Choosing bricks 21–2, Bonding bricks 26, Footings 27, Profile boards 27, Copings 30, Building piers 33, Gauge stick 65

Pointing brickwork

Pointing the mortar between the bricks makes for packed, watertight joints as well as enhancing the appearance of the wall. Well-struck joints and clean brickwork are essential if the wall is to look professionally built. For best results, the mortar must be shaped when it has just the right consistency.

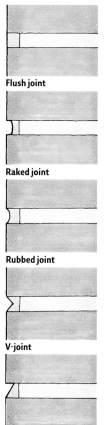

Flush joint

Raked joint

Rubbed joint

V-joint

Weatherstruck joint

Consistency of the mortar

If the mortar is still too wet, the joint will not be crisp and you may drag mortar out from between the bricks. On the other hand, if it's left to harden too long, pointing will be hard work and you may leave dark marks on the joint.

Test the consistency of the mortar by pressing your thumb into a joint. If it holds a clear impression without sticking to your thumb, the mortar is just right for pointing. Because it's important to start shaping the joints at exactly the right moment, you may have to point the work in stages before you can complete the wall. Shape the joints to match existing brickwork, or choose a profile that is suitable for the prevailing weather conditions.

Shaping the mortar joints

Flush joint
After using the edge of your trowel to scrape the mortar flush, stipple the joints with a stiff-bristle brush to expose the sand aggregate.

Raked joint
Use a piece of wood or metal to rake out the joints to a depth of about 6mm (¼in), then compress them again by smoothing the mortar lightly with a piece of rounded dowel rod. Raked joints do not shed water, so they are not suitable for exposed work.

Rubbed (concave) joint
Buy a shaped jointing tool to make a rubbed joint, or improvise with a length of bent tubing. Scrape the mortar flush first, then drag the tool along the joints. Finish the vertical joints, then shape the horizontal ones. This is a utilitarian joint, ideal for a wall built with second-hand bricks that are not good enough to take a crisp joint.

Weatherstruck joint
The angled weatherstruck joint will withstand harsh conditions. Use a small pointing trowel to shape the vertical joints (**1**) – they can slope to the left or right, but be consistent.

Shape the horizontal joints, allowing the mortar to spill out slightly at the base of each joint. Finish the joint by cutting off excess mortar with a tool called a Frenchman, which is rather like a table knife with its tip bent at 90 degrees. You can improvise one by bending a strip of metal. Make a neat, straight edge to the mortar, using a batten aligned with the bottom of each joint to guide the Frenchman (**2**); nail two scraps of wood to the batten to hold it away from the wall.

Brushing the brickwork
Let the shaped joints harden a little before cleaning scraps of mortar from the face of the wall with a medium-soft banister brush. Sweep the brush lightly across the joints to avoid damaging the mortar.

Shape the mortar with a jointing tool

V-joint
Produced in a similar way to the rubbed joint, the V-joint gives a smart finish to new brickwork and sheds rainwater well.

1 Shape a weatherstruck joint with a trowel

2 Remove excess mortar with a Frenchman

Coping brick walls

The coping – which forms the top course of the wall – protects the brickwork from weathering and gives the wall a finished appearance.

Integral coping
You could finish the wall by laying the last course frog downwards – but a coping of half bats laid on end looks more professional.

Brick coping
Specially shaped coping bricks are designed to shed rainwater.

Slab coping
Choose a stone or concrete slab that is wider than the wall.

Tile-and-brick coping
Lay roof tiles or special creasing tiles beneath a coping of bricks.

Technically, a coping that is flush with both faces of the wall is called a capping. A true coping projects from the face, so that water drips clear.

You can finish a wall with a coping of matching bricks or create a pleasing contrast with engineering bricks, which also offer superior water resistance. Alternatively, buy special coping bricks designed to shed rainwater.

Stone or cast-concrete slabs are popular for coping garden walls. Both are quick to lay and are usually wide enough to form low bench-type seating.

On an exposed site, consider installing a bituminous-felt DPC under the coping to reduce the risk of frost attack; or lay two courses of plain roof tiles with staggered joints and a brick coping above. Let the tiles project from the face of the wall, but run a sloping mortar joint along the top of the projection to shed water.

SEE ALSO > Engineering bricks 21

Building intersecting walls

When building new garden walls that intersect at right angles, either join them by bonding the brickwork (see below) or take the easier option and link them with wall ties at every third course. If the intersecting wall is more than 2m (6ft 6in) in length, make the junction a control joint by using straight metal strips as wall ties.

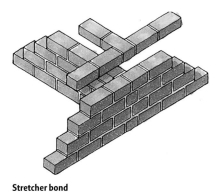

Stretcher bond

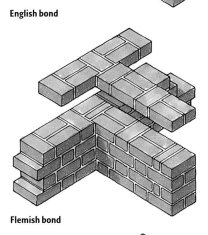

English bond

Flemish bond

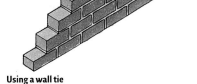

Using a wall tie

Building up to a wall

When building a new wall to intersect with an existing wall of a house, you must include a damp-proof course in order to prevent water bridging the house's DPC via the new masonry. You must also make a positive joint between the walls.

Inserting a DPC

The Building Regulations require a damp-proof course to be installed in all habitable buildings. This consists of a layer of impervious material built into the mortar bed 150mm (6in) above ground level. When you build a new wall, its DPC must coincide with the DPC in the existing structure. Use a roll of bituminous felt, chosen to match the thickness of the new wall.

Locate the house's DPC and build the first few courses of the new wall up to that level. Spread a thin bed of mortar on the bricks, and lay the DPC upon it with the end of the roll turned up against the existing wall. The next course of bricks will trap the DPC between the header joint and the wall. Lay more mortar on top of the DPC to produce a standard 10mm (³⁄₈in) joint, ready for laying the next course in the normal way. If you have to join rolls of DPC, overlap the ends by 150mm (6in).

Tying-in the new wall

The traditional method for linking a new wall with an existing structure involves chopping recesses in the brickwork at every fourth course. End bricks of the new wall are set into the recesses, bonding the two structures together. However, a simpler method is to bolt to the wall a stainless-metal connector designed to anchor bricks or concrete blocks, using special wall ties. Standard connectors will accommodate walls from 100 to 250mm (4 to 10in) thick.

Bolt a connector to the old wall, just above the DPC (**1**), using expanding bolts or stainless-steel coach screws and wallplugs. Mortar the end of a brick before laying it against the connector (**2**). At every third course, hook a wall tie into one of the lugs in the connector and bed each tie in the mortar joint (**3**).

Lap the existing DPC with the new roll

DPC on a sloping site
When the site slopes noticeably, the wall footing is stepped to keep the top of the wall level. If you include a DPC in the wall, that too must follow the line of the steps to keep it the required height above ground level.

1 Bolt the stainless-steel connector to the wall

2 Lay the bricks against the connector

3 Bed a special wall tie in the mortar joint

You can tooth a wall into the brickwork

Wall ties for attaching to the connector

SEE ALSO > Choosing bricks 21–2, Stepped footings 27, Bricklaying techniques 28, Wall ties 32, Control joints 33

Brick piers

A pier is a freestanding column of masonry that may be used, for example, as a support for a porch or a pergola or to form an individual gatepost. When a column is built as part of a wall, it is more accurately termed a pilaster. In practice, however, the word column is often used to mean either structure. To avoid confusion, any supporting brick column will be described here as a pier.

Structural considerations

Over a certain length and height (see below), a freestanding wall must be buttressed at regular intervals by piers. The wall's straight sections have to be tied to the piers, either by a brick bond or by inserting metal wall ties in every third course of bricks.

Whatever its height, any single-width brick wall would benefit from supporting piers at each end and at gateways, where it is most vulnerable. Piers also serve to improve the appearance of this type of wall.

Piers that are more than 1m (3ft 3in) high, especially those supporting gates, should be built around steel reinforcing rods set in the concrete footings.

Whether reinforcement is included or not, allow for the size of the piers when you are designing the footings.

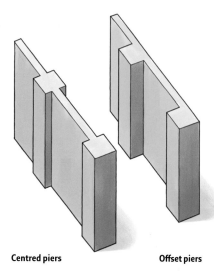

Centred piers   **Offset piers**

Wall ties
If you prefer the appearance of bonded-brick piers, construct them as shown below. It is easier, however, to use wall ties to reinforce continuous vertical joints in the brickwork, especially when you are building a wall centred on piers.

Designing the piers

Piers should be placed no more than 3m (9ft 9in) apart in walls over a certain height (see chart below). The wall itself can be flush with one face of each pier, but the structure is stronger if the wall is centred on the piers.

Piers should be a minimum of twice the thickness of a wall that is 102.5mm (4in) thick, but you need to build piers 328mm (1ft 1½in) square to buttress a wall 215mm (8½in) thick or when reinforcement is required – for gateways, for example.

INCORPORATING PIERS IN A BRICK WALL		
Thickness of wall	**Maximum height without piers**	**Maximum pier spacing**
102.5mm (4in)	450mm (1ft 6in)	3m (9ft 9in)
215mm (8½in)	1.35m (4ft 6in)	3m (9ft 9in)

Bonding piers
Although it's simpler to tie a wall to a pier with wall ties (see above), it is relatively easy to bond a pier into a wall that is of single-brick width.

Colour key
You will have to cut certain bricks to bond a pier into a straight wall. Whole bricks are coloured with a light tone; three-quarter bats with a medium tone; and half bats with a dark tone.

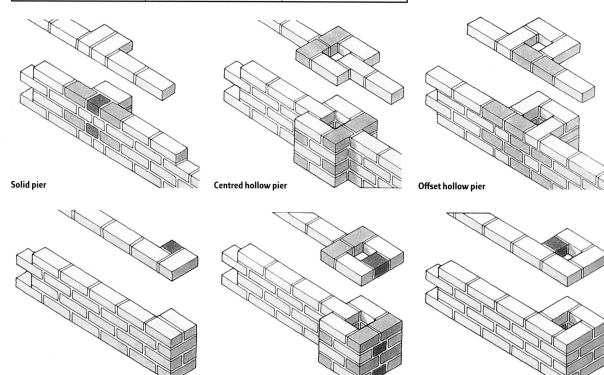

Solid pier   **Centred hollow pier**   **Offset hollow pier**

Solid end pier   **Centred hollow end pier**   **Offset hollow end pier**

SEE ALSO > Choosing bricks 21–2, Footings 27, Laying bricks 28–31

Building brick piers

Accurately mark out the positions of the piers on the concrete footing and then, between them, mark out the face of the wall itself.

Lay the first course of bricks for the piers, using a bricklayer's line stretched between two stakes to align them (**1**). Adjust the position of the line if necessary, and fill in between with the first straight course, working from both ends towards the middle (**2**). Build alternate pier and wall courses, checking that the bricks are laid level and the faces and corners of the piers are vertical. At every third course, push metal wall ties into the mortar bed to span the joints between the wall and piers (**3**). Continue in the same way to the required height of the wall, then raise the piers by at least one extra course (**4**). Lay a coping along the wall, and cap the piers with concrete or stone slabs (**5**).

1 Lay pier bases
Stretch a bricklayer's line to position the bases of the piers.

2 Lay first wall course
Use the line to ensure the first course of bricks is built perfectly straight.

3 Lay pier ties
Join the piers to the wall by inserting wall ties into every third course. Put a tie into alternate courses for a gate-supporting pier.

4 Raise the piers
Build the piers higher than the wall to allow for a decorative coping along the top course.

5 Lay the coping
Lay coping slabs and cap the piers.

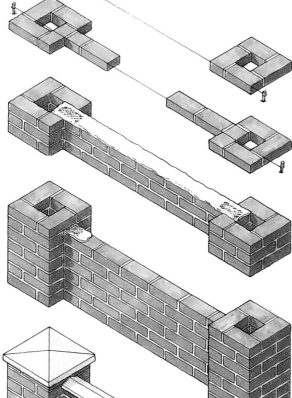

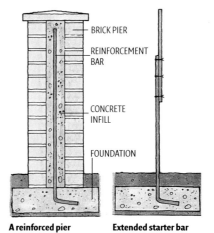

Positioning piers
This brick-built pier has been strategically placed to support the wall and disguise the junction where the ground level changes.

Control joints

A brick wall moves from time to time as a result of the expansion and contraction of the materials. Over short distances the movement has hardly any effect, but in a long wall it can crack the structure.

To compensate for this movement, build continuous unmortared vertical joints into the wall at intervals of about 6m (19ft 6in). Although these control joints can be placed in a straight section of walling, it is more convenient to place them where the wall meets a pier. Build the pier and wall as normal – but omit the mortar from the header joints of the wall. Instead of inserting standard wall ties, embed a galvanized strip, 3mm (⅛in) thick, in the mortar bed. Lightly grease one half of the strip with petroleum jelly – so that it can slide lengthwise to allow for movement and yet still key the wall and pier together. When the wall is complete, fill the joint from both sides with mastic.

Reinforcing a pier

Use 16mm (⅝in) steel reinforcing bars to strengthen brick piers. If the pier is less than 1m (3ft 3in) in height, use a single continuous length of bar; for taller piers, embed a bent 'starter' bar in the footing, projecting a minimum of 500mm (1ft 8in) above the level of the concrete. As the work proceeds, use galvanized wire to bind extension bars to the projection of the starter bar, up to within 50mm (2in) of the top of the pier. Fill in around the bar with concrete as you build the pier, packing it carefully to avoid disturbing the brickwork.

Control joint

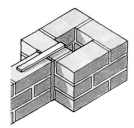

Making a control joint
When making a control joint, tie the pier to the wall with galvanized-metal strips (shown here before the bed of mortar is laid). Mastic is squeezed into the vertical joint between the wall and the pier.

BRICK PIER
REINFORCEMENT BAR
CONCRETE INFILL
FOUNDATION

A reinforced pier   **Extended starter bar**

SEE ALSO > Choosing bricks 21–2, Bricklaying techniques 28, Bricklayer's line 29, Setting out 29

Building with concrete blocks

Don't dampen concrete blocks before you lay them – since wet blocks may shrink and crack the mortar joints as the wall dries out. Block walls need the same type of concrete footings and mortar mixes as brickwork. Because concrete blocks are made in a greater variety of sizes, you can build a wall of any thickness, using a simple stretcher bond. Make the mortar joints flush with the surface of a wall that is to be rendered or plastered. For painted or exposed blockwork, point the joints using a style that is appropriate to the location and to enhance the appearance of the wall.

Colourful block walls
Paint-quality blocks decorated with smooth masonry paint make a welcome change from the usual monotonous grey concrete.

● **Building piers**
High freestanding garden walls constructed from blocks must be supported by piers at 3m (9ft 9in) intervals.

Building a partition wall

It is usual to divide up large interior spaces with non-loadbearing stud partitions; but if your house is built on a concrete pad, a practical alternative is to use concrete blocks. If you're going to install a doorway in the partition, plan its position to avoid cutting too many blocks. Allow for the wooden doorframe and lining, as well as a precast lintel to support the masonry above the opening. Fill the space above the lintel with concrete coursing bricks.

Bolt metal connectors to the existing structure in order to support each end of the new partition wall. Plumb the connectors accurately to make sure the new wall is built perfectly upright.

Lay the first course of blocks without mortar, across the room, to check their spacing and to determine the position of a doorway. Mark the positions of the blocks before building stepped leads at each end, as for brickwork. Check for accuracy with a spirit level, and then fill in between the leads with blocks.

Build another three courses, anchoring the end blocks to the connectors with wall ties in every joint. Leave the mortar to harden overnight before you continue.

Cutting blocks
Cut a block by scoring a line right round it, using a bolster chisel and straightedge. Deepen the line into a groove by striking the chisel sharply with a club hammer, working your way round the block until it fractures along the chiselled groove.

Cutting a concrete block

Building a partition

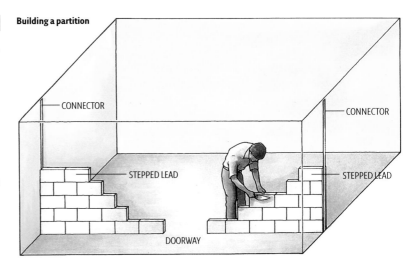

CONNECTOR   CONNECTOR   STEPPED LEAD   STEPPED LEAD   DOORWAY

Building intersecting garden walls

Butt intersecting garden walls together with a continuous vertical joint between them, but anchor the structure as for brickwork with wire-mesh wall ties. If you build a wall with heavyweight hollow blocks, use stout metal tie bars with a bend at each end. Fill the block voids with mortar to embed the ends of the bars. Install a tie in every course.

Control joints

Walls more than 6m (19ft 6in) long should be built with a continuous vertical control joint to allow for expansion. Place an unmortared joint in a straight section of wall or against a pier and bridge the gap with galvanized-metal strips, as for brickwork. Fill the vertical joint with flexible mastic.

If you need to insert a control joint in a partition wall, it's convenient to form the joint at a door opening – take it round one end of the lintel and then vertically to the ceiling. Having filled the joint with mortar in the normal way, rake it out to a depth of 18mm (¾in) on both sides of the wall, then fill flush with mastic.

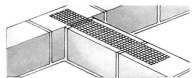

Wire-mesh wall ties for solid blocks

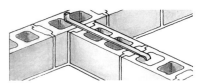

Metal tie bar for hollow blocks

Forming a control joint next to a door opening
On both sides of the wall, take the joint around the lintel and up to the ceiling.

SEE ALSO > Concrete blocks 23, Mixing mortar 25, Stretcher bond 26, Bricklaying techniques 28, Stepped leads 29, Pointing 30, Intersecting walls 31, Wall connectors 31, Control joints 33

Building with stone

Constructing garden walling with natural stone requires a different approach to building with bricks or concrete blocks. A stone wall has to be as stable as any other masonry wall, but its visual appeal relies on the coursing being less regular – indeed, there is no real coursing when a wall is built with undressed stone.

Designing the wall

A dry-stone wall must be 'battered' – in other words, it has to have a wide base and the sides must slope inwards. For a wall about 1m (3ft 3in) in height – it's dangerous to build a dry-stone wall any higher – the base should be no less than 450mm (1ft 6in) wide; and you need to provide a minimum slope of 25mm (1in) for every 600mm (2ft) of height.

Traditionally, the base of this type of wall rests on a bed of sand 100mm (4in) deep, laid on compacted soil at the bottom of a shallow trench. For a more reliable foundation, lay a 100mm (4in) concrete footing, making it about 100mm (4in) wider than the wall on each side.

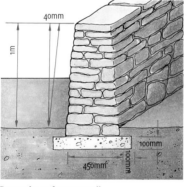

Proportions of a stone wall

Structural considerations

Not all stone walls are built with mortar, although it is often used with dressed or semi-dressed stone in order to provide additional stability.

Instead, many walls are tapered – with heavy flat stones laid at the base of the wall, followed by proportionally smaller stones as the height increases. This traditional form of construction was developed to prevent walls made with unmortared stones toppling sideways when subjected to high winds or the weight of farm animals.

Far from detracting from its appearance, the informality of this type of construction suits a country-style garden perfectly.

Building a dry-stone wall

A true dry-stone wall relies on a selective choice of stones and careful placement to provide stability. However, there's no reason why you can't introduce mortar, particularly within the core of the wall, and still maintain the appearance of dry-stone walling.

Another way to help stabilize a wall is to bed the stones in soil, packing it firmly into the crevices as you lay each course. This enables you to plant alpines or other rockery plants in the wall, even during construction.

When you are selecting the masonry, look out for flat stones in a variety of sizes and make sure you have some that are large enough to run the full width of the wall, especially at the base of the structure. Placed at regular intervals, these 'bonding' stones are important components, as they tie the loose rubble into a cohesive structure.

Constructing the wall

Assuming you're using soil as your jointing material, spread a 25mm (1in) layer over the footing and then place a substantial bonding stone across the width to form the bed of the first course (**1**). Lay other stones, about the same height as the bonding stone, along each side of the wall, pressing them down into the soil to make a firm base. It's worth stretching a bricklayer's line along each side of the wall to help you make a reasonably straight base.

Lay smaller stones between to fill out the base of the wall (**2**), then pack more soil into all the crevices.

Spread another layer of soil on top of the base and lay a second course of stones, bridging the joints between the stones below (**3**). Press the stones down firmly, so they lean inwards towards the centre of the wall. As you proceed, check by eye that the coursing is about level and remember to include bonding stones at regular intervals.

You can introduce plants into the larger crevices or hammer smaller stones into the chinks to lock large stones in place.

At the top of the wall, either fill the core with soil for plants or lay large, flat coping stones, balancing them with packed soil. Finally, brush loose soil from the wall faces.

Dry-stone wall
Traditional dry-stone walling is stable without having to fill the joints with mortar.

Pointed stonework
Mortar is required for buildings and substantial freestanding walls constructed from dressed or semi-dressed stone.

Reinforcing the wall
Hammer small stones into the gaps between the larger stones to lock them in place.

1 Lay a bonding stone across the end of the wall

2 Fill out the base with small stones

3 Lay a second course of stones

SEE ALSO > Natural stone 24, Footings 27, Bricklayer's line 29

Building low retaining walls

Retaining walls are designed to hold back a bank of earth, but don't attempt to cut into a steep bank and restrain it with a single high wall. Apart from the obvious dangers of the wall collapsing, terracing the slope with a series of low walls is a more attractive solution, as it offers opportunities for imaginative planting.

Choosing your materials

Both bricks and concrete blocks make sturdy retaining walls, provided that they are reinforced with metal bars buried in a sound concrete footing. Either run the bars through hollow concrete blocks or build a double skin of brickwork, rather like a miniature cavity wall, using wall ties to bind each skin together.

The mass and weight of natural stone make it ideal for retaining walls. A stone wall should be battered (see BUILDING WITH STONE) to an angle of 50mm (2in) for every 300mm (1ft) of height, to provide support for the bank. For safety, don't build higher than 1m (3ft 3in).

A skilful professional builder could construct a perfectly safe dry-stone retaining wall – but unless you have had sufficient experience, it is advisable to use mortar for additional rigidity.

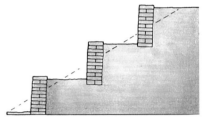

Terracing with retaining walls

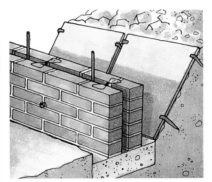

Retaining wall of hollow concrete blocks

Use two skins of brick tied together

Stone wall retaining a bank of earth

Constructing the wall

Excavate the soil to provide enough room to dig the footing and construct the wall. If the bank is loosely packed, restrain it temporarily with sheets of scrap plywood or corrugated iron. Drive metal pegs into the bank to hold the sheets in place (**1**). Lay the footing at the base of the bank, and allow it to set before you begin building the wall.

Use conventional techniques to build a block or brick wall. Lay uncut stones as if you were building a dry-stone wall, but set each course on mortar. If you use regular stone blocks, stagger the joints and select stones of different proportions to add variety to the wall. Bed the stones in mortar.

You must allow for drainage behind the wall, or the soil will become waterlogged. So when you lay the second course of stones, embed 22mm (¾in) plastic pipes in the mortar bed, sloping them slightly downwards away from the bank. Lay the pipes about 1m (3ft) apart, making sure that they pass right through the wall and project a little from the face (**2**).

Finishing a stone wall

When the wall is complete, rake out the joints so that it looks like a genuine dry-stone wall. An old paintbrush is a useful tool for smoothing the mortar in deep crevices, in order to make firm watertight joints. It is best to point regular stones with concave rubbed joints.

Allow the mortar to set hard before filling behind the wall. Lay hardcore at the base to cover the drainage pipes, and pack shingle against the wall as you replace the soil.

1 Hold back the earth with scrap boards

2 Set plastic pipes in the wall for drainage

TOPSOIL
SHINGLE
HARDCORE
DRAINAGE PIPE
FOOTING

Filling behind a stone wall

SEE ALSO > Footings 27, Laying bricks 28–33, Pointing 30, Reinforcing bars 33

Paths, drives and patios

For many people, paving of any kind is associated with the old 'back yard' environment, devoid of plants, trees and grass. But in reality, introducing paving into a garden provides an opportunity to create contrasts of colour and texture, which are intensified by sunlight and deep shade.

The marriage of different materials offers numerous possibilities. It may be convenient to define areas of paving as paths, drives or patios, but they are only names to describe the function of particular spaces in the garden. There's no reason why you cannot blend one area into another by using the same material throughout, or by employing similar colours to link one type of paving with another. On the other hand, you could take a completely different approach and deliberately juxtapose coarse and smooth textures or pale and dark tones to make one space stand out from the next.

Having so many choices at your disposal does have its drawbacks, as there's a strong temptation to experiment with any and every combination until the end result is a mishmash that's distracting to the eye. A few well-chosen materials that complement the house and its surroundings produce an effect that is far more appealing.

Paved patio
A paved area that's surrounded by walls built from stone or brick makes a perfect suntrap.

Sometimes a hard and unyielding surface can be softened by the addition of foliage. And plants that otherwise recede into a background of soil and grass are seen to advantage against stone and gravel.

SEE ALSO > Concrete mixes 41, Finishing concrete 45, Paving slabs 46

Working with concrete

Concrete is more versatile than some people imagine. It may appear to be a rather drab, utilitarian material for the garden, but you can add texture and colour to ordinary concrete or make good use of one of the many types of cast-concrete slabs and bricks made for paving patios, paths and driveways.

Storing materials

If you buy sand and aggregate in sacks, use as much as you require for the job and keep the rest bagged up until you need it again. Loose ingredients should be piled separately on a hard surface or on thick polythene sheets. Cover the piles with weighted sheets of plastic.

Storing cement is more critical. It's usually sold in paper sacks, which will absorb moisture from the ground – so pile them on a board propped up on battens. It's best to keep cement in a dry shed or garage; but if you have to store it outdoors, cover the bags with sheets of plastic weighted down with bricks.

Once a bag is opened, cement will absorb moisture from the air, so keep a partly used bag in a sealed plastic sack.

Storing ingredients
Use a plank of wood to separate piles of sand and aggregate. Keep bags of cement under cover.

Ingredients of concrete

In its simplest form, concrete consists of cement and fine particles of stone (sand and pebbles) known as aggregate. The dry ingredients are mixed with water to create a chemical reaction with the cement, which binds the aggregate into a hard, dense material.

The initial hardening process takes place quite quickly. But although the mix becomes unworkable after a couple of hours, depending on the temperature and humidity, the concrete has no real strength for 3 to 7 days.

The hardening process continues for up to a month, or as long as there is moisture still present within the concrete. Moisture is essential to the reaction; consequently, concrete must not be allowed to dry out too quickly during the first few days.

Cement
Standard Portland cement, sold in 50kg (110lb) bags, is used in the manufacture of concrete. In its dry condition, it is a fine grey powder.

In some areas of the country, the soil contains soluble sulphates that are harmful to concrete (your local Building Control Officer can advise you about this). If necessary, use special sulphate-resisting Portland cement.

Sand
Sharp sand – a rather coarse and gritty material – constitutes part of the aggregate of a concrete mix. Don't buy fine builder's sand (used for mortar); and avoid unwashed or beach sand, both of which contain impurities that can affect the quality of the concrete.

Builders' merchants sell sharp sand loose by the cubic metre (or cubic yard). However, it is often more convenient to buy it packed in large plastic bags if you have to transport it by car or van.

Coarse aggregate
Coarse aggregate is gravel or crushed stone composed of particles large enough to be retained by a 5mm (¼in) sieve, up to a maximum size of 20mm (¾in) for normal use. Once again, it can be bought loose by the cubic metre (cubic yard) or in smaller quantities packed in plastic sacks.

Pigments
Special pigments can be added to a concrete mix in order to colour it, but it's difficult to guarantee an even colour from one batch to another.

Combined aggregate
Naturally occurring sand-and-gravel mix – known as ballast – is sold as a combined aggregate for concreting. The proportion of sand to gravel is not guaranteed unless the ballast has been reconstituted to adjust the mix, so you may need to do this yourself. In any case, make sure the ballast has been washed thoroughly to remove any impurities.

Dry-packed concrete
You can buy dry cement mixed with sand and aggregate in the required proportions for making concrete. Choose the proportion that best suits the job you have in mind. Fast-setting concrete for erecting fence posts is one typical ready-mixed product.

Concrete mix is sold in various-size bags up to 50kg (110lb). Available from the usual outlets, this is a more expensive way of buying concrete ingredients, but it's a simple and convenient method of ordering exactly the amount you need. Before you add water, make sure the ingredients are mixed thoroughly.

Water
Use ordinary tap water. Impurities and salt contained in river or sea water are detrimental to concrete.

PVA admixture
You can buy a PVA admixture from builders' merchants to make a smoother concrete mix that is less susceptible to frost damage. Follow the manufacturers' instructions for its use.

SEE ALSO > Calculating quantities 41, Cleaning equipment 43, Laying concrete 42–5

Mixing concrete

Hire a small mixing machine if you need to prepare a large volume of concrete, but for the average job it's perhaps more convenient to mix it by hand. It isn't necessary to weigh the ingredients – simply mix them by volume, choosing the proportions that suit the job in hand.

Mixing by hand

Use two large buckets to measure the ingredients, one for the cement and – in order to keep the cement perfectly dry – another, identical, bucket for the sand and coarse aggregate. Using two shovels is also a good idea.

Measure the materials accurately, levelling them with the rim of the bucket. Tap the side of the bucket with the shovel as you load it with sand or cement, so that the loose particles are shaken down.

Mix the sand and coarse aggregate first, on a hard, flat surface. Scoop a depression in the pile for the measure of cement, and mix all the ingredients until they form an even colour.

Form another depression and add some water from a watering can. Push the dry ingredients into the water from around the edge (**1**) until the surface water has been absorbed, then mix the batch by chopping the concrete with the shovel. Add more water, then turn the concrete from the bottom of the pile and chop it as before until the whole batch has an even consistency.

To test the workability of the mix, form a series of ridges by dragging the back of the shovel across the pile (**2**). The surface of the concrete should be flat and even in texture, and the ridges should hold their shape without slumping.

1 Push the dry ingredients into the water

2 Make ridges with the shovel

Mixing by machine

Make sure you set up the concrete mixer on a hard, level surface and that the drum is upright before you start the motor. Use a bucket to pour half the measure of coarse aggregate into the drum and add water. Add the sand and cement alternately in small batches, plus the rest of the aggregate. Keep on adding water little by little along with the other ingredients.

Let the batch mix for a few minutes. Then tilt the drum of the mixer while it is still rotating and turn out some of the concrete into a wheelbarrow, so you can test its consistency (see above). If necessary, return the concrete to the mixer to adjust it.

Machine safety

When you hire a concrete mixer, take time to read the safety advice that's supplied with the machine.

● Make sure you understand the operating instructions before you turn the machine on.

● Prop the mixer with blocks of woods until it is level and stable.

● Never put your hands or shovel into the drum while the mixer is running.

● Don't lean over a rotating drum to inspect the contents.

● It is advisable to wear goggles when mixing concrete.

Ready-mixed concrete

If you need a lot of concrete for a driveway or large patio, it may be worth ordering a delivery of ready-mixed concrete from a local supplier.

Always contact the supplier well in advance to discuss your particular requirements. Specify the proportions of the ingredients, and say whether you require a retarding agent to slow down the setting time. (Once a normal mix of concrete is delivered, you will have about 2 hours in which to finish the job. A retarding agent can add a couple of hours to the setting time.) Tell the supplier exactly what you need the concrete for, and accept his advice. For quantities of less than 6cu m (8cu yd), you may find you have to shop around for a supplier who is willing to deliver without making an additional charge.

In order to avoid moving the concrete too far by wheelbarrow, you will want it discharged as close to the site as possible, if not directly into place. However, the chute on a delivery truck can reach only so far, and if the vehicle is too large or heavy to drive onto your property you will need several helpers to move the concrete while it is still workable. A single cubic metre of concrete will fill 25 to 30 large wheelbarrows. If it takes longer than 30 to 40 minutes to discharge the load, you may have to pay extra.

Professional mixing

There are companies who will deliver concrete ingredients and mix them to your specifications on the spot. All you have to do is barrow the concrete and pour it into place. There's no waste, as you pay only for the concrete you use. Telephone a local company for details on price and minimum quantity.

Ready-mixed concrete can be delivered directly to your home

SEE ALSO > Calculating quantities 41, Cleaning equipment 43, Laying concrete 42–5

Designing concrete paving

The notion of having to design simple concrete pads and pathways may seem odd, but there are important factors to consider if the concrete is to be durable. At the least, you will have to decide on the thickness of the concrete that is needed to support the weight of traffic, and the angle of slope required to drain off surface water.

When an area of concrete is large or if it's a complicated shape, you need to incorporate control joints to allow the material to expand and contract. If a pad is for a habitable building, then it must include a damp-proof membrane to prevent moisture rising from the ground. Even the proportions of sand, cement and aggregate used in the mix have to be considered carefully.

Deciding on the slope

● **Sloping floors**
Although you can build upon a perfectly flat base, it is a good idea to slope the floor towards the door of a garage or outbuilding that is to be scrubbed out from time to time. Alternatively, slope a floor in two directions towards the middle to form a shallow drain that runs to the door.

A freestanding pad can be laid perfectly level, especially when it's supporting a small outbuilding – but a very slight slope or fall will prevent water collecting in puddles if you have failed to get the concrete absolutely flat. If a pad is laid directly against a house, it must have a definite fall away from the building; and any parking area or drive must shed water to provide adequate traction for vehicles and to minimize the formation of ice. When concrete is laid against a building, it must be at least 150mm (6in) below the existing damp-proof course.

USE OF PAVING	ANGLE OF FALL
Pathways	Not required.
Drive	1 in 40 (25mm per metre, 1in per yard)
Patio Parking space	1 in 60 away from the building (16mm per metre, ⅝in per yard)
Pads for garages and outbuildings	1 in 80 towards the door (12.5mm per metre, ½in per yard)

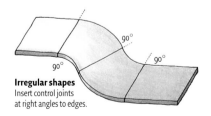

Irregular shapes
Insert control joints at right angles to edges.

Recommended thicknesses for concrete

The normal thicknesses recommended for concrete paving assume it will be laid on a firm subsoil. If the soil is clay or peat, increase the thickness by about 50 per cent. The same applies to a new site, where the soil may not be compacted.

Unless the concrete is for pedestrian traffic only, lay a subbase of compacted hardcore below the paving. This will absorb ground movement without affecting the concrete itself. A subbase is not essential for a very lightweight structure, such as a small wooden shed; but in case you want to increase the weight at some time in the future, it is wisest to install a subbase at the outset.

Pathways
For pedestrian traffic only:
Concrete: 75mm (3in)
Subbase: Not required

Patios
Any extensive area of concrete for pedestrian traffic:
Concrete: 100mm (4in)
Subbase: 100mm (4in)

Driveways
Drive used for an average family car only:
Concrete: 125mm (5in)
Subbase: 150mm (6in)
For heavier vehicles, such as delivery trucks:
Concrete: 150mm (6in)
Subbase: 150mm (6in)

Lightweight structures
Support pad for a wooden shed, coal bunker and so on:
Concrete: 75mm (3in)
Subbase: 75mm (3in)

Parking space
Exposed paving for parking family car:
Concrete: 125mm (5in)
Subbase: 150mm (6in)

Garage
Thicken up the edges of a garage pad to support the weight of the walls:
Concrete:
Floor: 125mm (5in)
Edges: 200mm (8in)
Subbase:
Minimum 150mm (6in)

Allowing for expansion

Changes in temperature cause concrete to expand and contract. If this movement is allowed to happen at random, then a pad or pathway will crack at the weakest or most vulnerable point.

Control joints composed of a compressible material will either absorb the movement or concentrate the force in predetermined areas where it will do little harm. The joints should meet the sides of a concrete area at more or less 90 degrees. Always place a control joint between concrete and a wall, and around inspection chambers.

Positioning control joints
The exact position of the control joints will depend on the area and shape of the concrete pad, path or driveway.

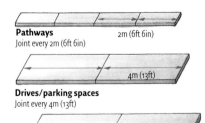

Pathways
Joint every 2m (6ft 6in)
2m (6ft 6in)
4m (13ft)

Drives/parking spaces
Joint every 4m (13ft)
4m (13ft)

Concrete pads
Joints no more than 4m (13ft) apart and around inspection chambers

Divide a pad into equal bays if:
● the length is more than twice the width
● the longest dimension is more than 40 times the thickness
● the longest dimension exceeds 4m (13ft)

SEE ALSO > Laying subbase 43, Control joints 44

Calculating quantities

To estimate the amount of materials that will be required, you need to calculate the volume of concrete in the finished pad, path or drive. Measure the surface area of the site, and multiply that figure by the thickness of the concrete.

Estimating quantities of concrete

Use the gridded diagram below to estimate the volume of concrete you will need.

Read off the area of the site in square metres (square yards) and trace it across horizontally to meet the angled line indicating the thickness of the concrete. Trace the line up to find the volume in cubic metres (cubic yards).

VOLUME OF CONCRETE REQUIRED

| Cu yd | 1 | 2 | 3 | 4 | 5 | 6 |
| Cu m | 1 | 2 | 3 | 4 | 5 |

THICKNESS

Sq yd / Sq m / AREA TO BE CONCRETED

Garage-pad edges: 200mm (8in)
Heavy-vehicle drives: 150mm (6in)
Car-parking, drives and garage floors: 125mm (5in)
Patios: 100mm (4in)
Pathways and light structures: 75mm (3in)

Estimating quantities of ingredients

Use the bar chart below to estimate the quantities of cement, sand and aggregate you will require to mix the volume of concrete arrived at by using the chart above.

The figures are based on the quantity of ingredients required to mix one cubic metre of concrete for a particular type of mix, plus about 10 per cent to allow for wastage.

		CUBIC METRES OF CONCRETE								
		1.00	1.50	2.00	2.50	3.00	3.50	4.00	4.50	5.00
GENERAL-PURPOSE MIX										
	Cement (50kg bags)	7.00	10.50	14.00	17.50	21.00	24.50	28.00	31.50	35.00
plus	Sand (cubic metres)	0.50	0.75	1.00	1.25	1.50	1.75	2.00	2.25	2.50
	Aggregate (cubic metres)	0.75	1.15	1.50	1.90	2.25	2.65	3.00	3.40	3.75
or	Ballast (cubic metres)	0.90	1.35	1.80	2.25	2.70	3.15	3.60	4.05	4.50
FOUNDATION MIX										
	Cement (50kg bags)	6.00	9.00	12.00	15.00	18.00	21.00	24.00	27.00	30.00
plus	Sand (cubic metres)	0.55	0.80	1.10	1.40	1.65	1.95	2.20	2.50	2.75
	Aggregate (cubic metres)	0.75	1.15	1.50	1.90	2.25	2.65	3.00	3.40	3.75
or	Ballast (cubic metres)	1.00	1.50	2.00	2.50	3.00	3.50	4.00	4.50	5.00
PAVING MIX										
	Cement (50kg bags)	9.00	13.50	18.00	22.50	27.00	31.50	36.00	40.50	45.00
plus	Sand (cubic metres)	0.45	0.70	0.90	1.15	1.35	1.60	1.80	2.00	2.25
	Aggregate (cubic metres)	0.75	1.15	1.50	1.90	2.25	2.65	3.00	3.40	3.75
or	Ballast (cubic metres)	1.00	1.50	2.00	2.50	3.00	3.50	4.00	4.50	5.00

Calculating areas

Squares and rectangles
Calculate the area of rectangular paving by multiplying width by length.

Example:
2m x 3m = 6sq m
78in x 117in = 9126sq in or 7sq yd

Circles
Use the formula πr^2 to calculate the area of a circle (π = 3.14, r = radius of the circle).

Example:
3.14 x 2sq m = 3.14 x 4 = 12.56sq m
3.14 x 78sq in = 3.14 x 6084 = 19104sq in or 14.75sq yd

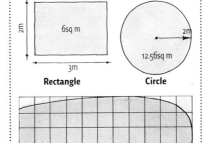

2m / 6sq m / 3m
Rectangle

2m / 12.56sq m
Circle

Irregular shapes
Draw an irregular area of paving on squared paper. To find the approximate area, count the whole squares and average out the portions.

SEE ALSO > Ingredients of concrete 38, Mixing concrete 39

Laying a concrete pad

Laying a simple pad as a base for a small shed or similar structure involves all the basic principles of concreting – including building a retaining formwork, as well as pouring, levelling and finishing the concrete. Provided that the base is less than 2m (6ft 6in) square, there's no need to include control joints.

Mixing concrete by volume

Whatever container you use to measure out the ingredients (shovel, bucket or wheelbarrow), the proportions remain the same.

MIXING CONCRETE BY VOLUME			
Type of mix		Proportions	For 1cu m concrete
GENERAL PURPOSE			
Use in most situations including covered pads other than garage floors.	**plus**	1 part cement	6.4 bags (50kg)
		2 parts sand	0.448cu m
		3 parts aggregate	0.672cu m
	or	4 parts ballast	0.896cu m
FOUNDATION			
Use for footings at the base of masonry walls.	**plus**	1 part cement	5.6 bags (50kg)
		2½ parts sand	0.49cu m
		3½ parts aggregate	0.686cu m
	or	5 parts ballast	0.98cu m
PAVING			
Use for parking areas, drives, pathways, and garage floors.	**plus**	1 part cement	8 bags (50kg)
		1½ parts sand	0.42cu m
		2½ parts aggregate	0.7cu m
	or	3½ parts ballast	0.98cu m

Excavating the site

First, mark out the area of the concrete pad with string lines attached to pegs driven into the ground outside the work area (**1**). Then remove the lines to excavate the site, but replace them afterwards to help position the formwork that will hold the concrete in place.

Remove the topsoil and all vegetable matter within the site down to a level that allows for the combined thickness of concrete and subbase. Extend the area of excavation about 150mm (6in)

outside the space allowed for the pad. Cut back any roots you encounter and, if there's any turf, put it aside to cover the infill surrounding the completed pad. Finally, level the bottom of the excavation by dragging a board across it and compact the soil with a garden roller.

Erecting the formwork

Until the concrete sets hard, it must be supported all round by formwork. For a straightforward rectangular pad, construct the formwork from softwood planks, 25mm (1in) thick, set on edge. The planks, which must be as wide as the finished depth of concrete, need to be held in place temporarily with stout 50 x 50mm (2 x 2in) wooden stakes. Second-hand or sawn timber is quite adequate. If it is slightly thinner than 25mm (1in), just use more stakes to brace it. If you have to join planks, butt them end to end, nailing a cleat on the outside.

Using the string lines as a guide, erect one board at the 'high' end of the pad and drive stakes behind it at about 1m (3ft) intervals or less, with one for each corner. The tops of the stakes and board must be level and need to correspond to the proposed surface of the pad exactly. Nail the board to the stakes (**2**).

Set up another board opposite the first one – but before you nail it to the stakes, establish the crossfall with a spirit level and straightedge. Work out the difference in level from one side of the pad to the other. For example, a pad that is 2m (6ft 6in) wide should drop 25mm (1in) over that distance. Tape a shim of timber to one end of the straightedge and, with the shim resting on the 'low' stakes, place the other end on the opposite board (**3**). Drive home each low stake until the spirit level reads horizontal, and then nail the board flush with the tops of the stakes.

Erect the ends of the formwork. Allowing the boards to overshoot at the corners will make it easier to dismantle them when the concrete has set (**4**). Use the straightedge, this time without the shim, to level the boards across the formwork.

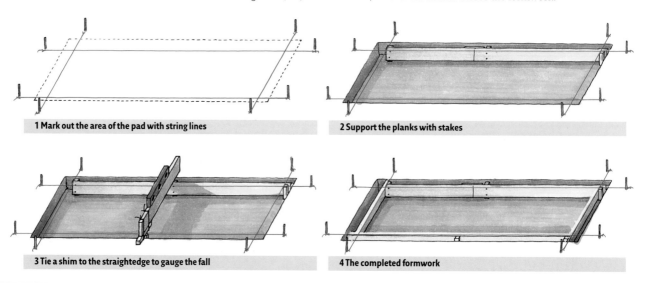

1 Mark out the area of the pad with string lines

2 Support the planks with stakes

3 Tie a shim to the straightedge to gauge the fall

4 The completed formwork

SEE ALSO >Ingredients of concrete 38, Deciding on the slope 40, Pad thickness 40, Finishing concrete 45, Control joints 44

Laying the subbase

Hoggin, a natural mixture of gravel and sand, is an ideal material for a subbase – but you can use crushed stone or brick, provided you throw out any plaster, scrap metal or similar rubbish. Also remove large lumps of masonry, as they will not compact well. Pour hardcore into the formwork and rake it fairly level before tamping it down with a heavy balk of timber (**5**). If there are any stubborn lumps, break them up with a heavy hammer. Fill in low spots with more hardcore or sharp sand until the subbase comes up to the underside of the formwork boards.

Filling with concrete

Mix the concrete as near to the site as is practicable and transport the fresh mix to the formwork in a wheelbarrow. Set up firm runways of scaffold boards if the ground is soft, especially around the perimeter of the formwork.

Dampen the subbase and formwork with a fine spray, and let surface water evaporate before tipping the concrete in place. Start filling from one end of the site and push the concrete firmly into the corners (**6**). Rake it level until the concrete stands about 18mm (¾in) above the level of the boards.

Tamp down the concrete with the edge of a plank, 50mm (2in) thick, that is long enough to reach across the formwork. Starting at one end of the site, compact the concrete with steady blows of the plank, moving it along by about half its thickness each time. Cover the whole area twice and then remove excess concrete, using the plank with a sawing action (**7**). Fill any low spots, then compact and level the concrete once more.

To retain the moisture, cover the pad with sheets of polythene, taped at the joints and weighted down with bricks around the edge. Alternatively, use wet sacking and keep it damp for 3 days, using a fine spray. Try to avoid laying concrete in very cold weather; but if that's unavoidable, spread a layer of earth or sand on top of the sheeting to insulate the concrete from frost.

It's perfectly safe to walk on the concrete after 3 days, but leave it for about a week before removing the formwork and erecting a shed or similar outbuilding.

Finishing the edges

If any of the edges of a concrete pad are exposed, the sharp corners could cause a painful injury – so radius the corners with an edging float. Run the float along the formwork as you finish the surface of the concrete.

This type of float is not expensive, but if you have difficulty obtaining one, you can make a float from thin sheet metal. Bend the piece of metal over a rod or tube, 18mm (¾in) in diameter, and then screw a wood batten to form a handle in the centre.

5 Level the hardcore base with a heavy balk of timber

6 Pour the concrete, starting in one corner

7 Use a sawing action to remove excess concrete

Extending a pad
If you want to enlarge your patio, simply butt a new section of concrete against the existing pad. The butt joint will in itself serve as a control joint. To add a narrow strip to a pad (so that you can erect a larger shed, for example), drill holes in the edge of the pad and use epoxy adhesive to glue in short reinforcing rods before pouring the fresh concrete.

Radius the corner, using an edging float

Cleaning tools and machinery

At the end of a working day wash all traces of concrete from your tools and wheelbarrow. When you have finished using a concrete mixer, add a few shovels of coarse aggregate and a little water, then run the machine for a couple of minutes to scour the inside of the drum. Dump the aggregate, then hose out the drum with clean water.

Shovel unused concrete into sacks, ready for disposal at a refuse dump, and wash the mixing area with a stiff broom. Never hose concrete or any of the separate ingredients into a drain.

SEE ALSO > Mixing concrete 39

Laying paths and drives

Paths and drives are laid and compacted in the same way as rectangular pads, using similar formwork to contain the concrete. However, the proportions of most paths and drives make the inclusion of control joints essential, to allow for expansion and contraction. You will have to install a subbase beneath a drive, but a pathway can be laid on compacted soil levelled with sharp sand. Establish a slight fall across the site to shed rainwater.

Setting out paths and drives

A sloping drive
If you build a drive on a sloping site, make the transition from level ground as gentle as possible. If the drive runs towards a garage, make the last 2m (6ft) slope up towards the door. Use a pole to impress a drain across the wet concrete at the lowest point.

Excavate the site, allowing for the thickness of the subbase and concrete. Level the bottom of the excavation, using a board to scrape the surface flat.

Drive accurately levelled pegs into the ground along the site, to act as datum points for the formwork. Space them about 2m (6ft 6in) apart along the centre of the pathway. Drive in the first peg until its top corresponds exactly to the proposed surface of the concrete. Use either a water level or a long straightedge and spirit level to position every other peg.

To make a water level, push a short length of transparent plastic tubing into each end of an ordinary garden hose. Holding both

ends together, fill the hose with water until it appears in the tube at both ends. Then mark the level on both tubes. As long as the ends remain open, the water level at each end is constant – enabling you to establish a level over any distance, even around corners. When you move the hose, cork each end to retain the water.

Tie one end of the hose to the first datum peg, ensuring that the marked level aligns with the top of the peg. Use the other end to establish the level of every other peg along the pathway. To set a fall with a water level, make a mark on one tube below the surface of the water and use that as a gauge for the top of the peg.

A water level made from a garden hose

Erecting formwork

Construct formwork from planks 25mm (1in) thick, as for a concrete pad. To check for level, rest a straightedge on the nearest datum peg (**1**).

If the drive or path is very long, it may be cheaper to hire metal 'road forms'. Straight-sided formwork is made from rigid units, but flexible sections are available to form curves. If you want to bend wooden formwork, make a series of closely spaced, parallel sawcuts across the width of the plank in the area of the curve.

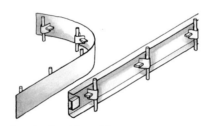

Curved and straight road forms

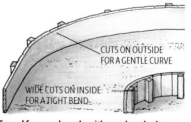

CUTS ON OUTSIDE FOR A GENTLE CURVE

WIDE CUTS ON INSIDE FOR A TIGHT BEND

Curved formwork made with wooden planks

Installing control joints

Install a permanent expansion joint every 2m (6ft 6in) for a pathway, and every 4m (13ft) along a drive. For a patio, you can install similar joints or use alternate-bay construction (see opposite).

Cut strips of either rot-proofed hardboard or softwood 12mm (½in) thick to fit exactly between the formwork and to match the depth of the concrete. Before pouring, hold the control joints in place with mounds of concrete and nails driven into the formwork on each side of the board (**2**).

As you fill the formwork, pack more concrete on both sides of each joint and tamp towards each joint from both sides, so that it is not dislodged.

On a narrow path, to prevent the concrete cracking between joints, cut grooves 18mm (¾in) deep across the compacted concrete to form dummy joints alternating with the physical ones. The simplest method is to cut a length of T-section metal to fit between the formwork boards. Place the strip on the surface of the wet concrete and tap it down with a mallet (**3**). Carefully lift the strip out of the concrete to leave a neat impression. If the concrete should move, a crack will develop unnoticed at the bottom of the groove.

Place strips of thick bituminous felt between concrete and an adjoining wall to absorb expansion. Hold the felt in place with mounds of concrete (as described above) before pouring the full amount of concrete into the site.

1 Level the formwork, using a datum peg

2 Support board with concrete and nails

3 Make a dummy joint with T-section metal

SEE ALSO > Control joints 40, Crossfall 40, Pad thickness 40, Formwork 42, Tamping concrete 43

Alternate-bay method

It is not always possible to lay all the concrete in a single operation – in which case, it's easier to divide the formwork crosswise with additional planks, known as 'stop ends', to create equal-size bays.

By filling alternate bays with concrete, you have plenty of time to compact and level each section and more room in which to manoeuvre. It is a convenient way to lay a large patio, for example, and it is the only method you can use for drives or paths that butt against a wall. Alternate-bay construction is also frequently used for building a drive on a steep slope, to prevent the heavy wet concrete from slumping downhill.

There is no need to install control joints when using bay construction, but you may want to form dummy joints for a neat appearance (see opposite).

Laying concrete next to a wall

Stand in the empty bays so you can compact concrete laid against a wall. When the first bays have set hard, remove the stop ends and fill the gaps, using the surface of the firm concrete as a level. Don't drive or park a vehicle on a concrete drive for 10 days after laying.

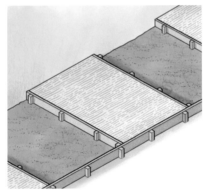

Construct bays when laying concrete next to a wall

Inspection chambers

Guard against expansion damaging an inspection chamber by surrounding it with control joints. Place formwork around the chamber and fill with concrete. When it's set, remove the boards and place either felt strips or preserver-treated softwood boards on all sides.

Surround an inspection chamber with formwork

SEE ALSO > Control joints 40, Tamping concrete 43

Surface finishes

The surface finishes produced by tamping or striking off with a sawing action are perfectly adequate for a workmanlike skid-proof surface for a pad, drive or pathway – but you can produce a range of other finishes once you have compacted and levelled the concrete.

Float finishes

You can smooth the tamped concrete by sweeping a wooden float across the surface, or make an even finer texture by finishing with a plasterer's trowel (steel float). Let the concrete dry out a little before using a float, or you will bring water to the top and weaken it – which will eventually result in a dusty residue on the hardened concrete. Bridge the formwork with a stout plank so that you can reach the centre, or hire a skip float with a long handle for large pads.

Brush finishes

To produce a finely textured surface, you can draw a yard broom across the setting concrete. Flatten the concrete initially with a wooden float and then make parallel passes with the broom, held at a low angle in order to avoid 'tearing' the surface.

Exposed-aggregate finish

Embedding small stones or pebbles in the surface makes a very attractive and practical finish, although you will need a little practice in order to do it successfully.

Scatter dampened pebbles onto the freshly laid concrete, and tamp them firmly with a block of timber till they are flush with the surface (**1**). Place a plank across the formwork and apply your full weight to make sure the surface is even. Leave it to harden for a while until all the surface water has evaporated, then use a very fine spray and a brush to wash away the cement from around the pebbles until they protrude (**2**). Cover the concrete for about 24 hours, then lightly wash the surface again to clean any sediment off the pebbles. Cover the concrete again, and leave it to harden thoroughly.

1 Tamp pebbles into fresh concrete

2 Wash the cement from around the pebbles

Removing oil stains
Oil and fuel spills can spoil the appearance of concrete drives and parking spaces. Using a stiff-bristle brush, scrub individual stains with a proprietary drive cleaner; and then 20 minutes later wash the concrete with a diluted solution of the same cleaner. Finally, hose the drive or parking space with clean water.

Paving slabs

Paving slabs are made either by hydraulic pressing or by casting in moulds to create the desired finish. Pigments and selected aggregates added to the concrete mix are used to create the illusion of a range of muted colours or natural stone. Combining two or more colours or textures within the same area of paving can be very striking.

Regular or informal paving
Constructing a simple grid from square slabs (left) is relatively easy. Although mixed paving (below) is more difficult to lay, it is richer in texture, colour and shape.

Shapes and sizes

Although some manufacturers offer a wider choice than others, there's a fairly standard range of shapes and modular sizes. It is usually possible to carry the largest slabs without help, but it's a good idea to get an assistant to help manoeuvre them carefully into place.

Square and rectangular

A single size and shape can be employed to make grid-like patterns or, when staggered, to create a bonded-brickwork effect. Use rectangular slabs to form a basket-weave or herringbone pattern. Alternatively, combine different sizes so as to create the impression of random paving, or mix slabs with a different type of paving to create a colourful contrast. Mixing slabs in this way requires a degree of restraint to prevent a paved area looking uncoordinated – but if you get it right, the result can be a feast for the eye.

Hexagonal slabs
Hexagonal slabs form honeycomb patterns. You can use half slabs to edge areas that are paved in straight lines.

Half-hexagonal slabs

Honeycomb pattern

Tapered slabs
Use tapered slabs to edge ponds and for encircling trees or making curved steps. Progressively larger slabs can be used for laying circular areas of paving.

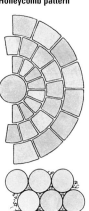

Circular slabs
Circular slabs make perfect individual stepping stones across a lawn or flower bed, but for a wide area fill the spaces between with cobbles or gravel.

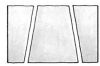

Butted circular slabs

SEE ALSO > Brick pavers 51

Laying paving slabs

Although laying paving slabs involves a good deal of physical labour, in terms of technique it's no more complicated than tiling a wall. Accurate setting out and careful laying, especially during the early stages, will help you achieve perfect results.

Setting out the area of paving

Wherever feasible, plan an area of paving so that it can be laid with whole slabs only. This eliminates the arduous task of cutting units to fit. Use pegs and string to mark out the perimeter of the paved area, and check the measurements before you excavate.

You can use a straight wall as a datum line and measure away from the wall. Or if the location dictates that you have to lay slabs near the house, allow for a 100 to 150mm (4 to 6in) margin of gravel between the paving and wall. A gravel margin not only saves time and money by using fewer slabs, but also provides an area for planting climbers and for adequate drainage to keep the wall dry.

Even so, establish a slope of 16mm per metre (⅝in per yard) across the paving, so that most of the surface water will drain into the garden. Any paving must be 150mm (6in) below a damp-proof course, in order to protect the building.

As paving slabs are made to fairly precise dimensions, marking out an area simply involves accurate measurement, allowing for a 6 to 10mm (¼ to ⅜in) gap between the slabs. Some slabs are cast with sloping edges to provide a tapered joint and should be butted edge to edge.

Preparing a base for the paving

Paving slabs must be laid upon a firm, level base, but the depth and substance of that base depend on the type of soil and the proposed use of the paving.

For straightforward patios and paths, remove vegetable matter and topsoil to allow for the thickness of the slabs, plus a 35mm (1½in) layer of sharp sand and an extra 18mm (¾in) – so the paving will be below the level of surrounding turf, in order to prevent damage to your lawn mower. Compact the soil with a garden roller, and then spread the sand with a rake and level it by scraping and tamping with a length of timber.

To support heavier loads, or if the soil is composed of clay or peat, lay a subbase of firmly compacted hardcore – broken bricks or crushed stone – to a depth of 75 to 100mm (3 to 4in) before spreading the sand to level the surface. If you plan to park vehicles on the paving, increase the depth of hardcore to 150mm (6in).

Cutting paving slabs

It is often necessary to trim concrete paving slabs to size in order to fit narrow margins.

Mark a line across a slab with chalk or a soft pencil. Place the slab on a bed of sand and, wearing plastic goggles, use a bolster and hammer to chisel a groove about 3mm (⅛in) deep along the line.

Turn the slab face down and, with the hammer, tap firmly along the groove until the slab splits. If need be, clean up the edge with a bolster.

To obtain a perfect cut, hire an angle grinder fitted with a stone-cutting disc.

Using an angle grinder
An angle grinder makes short work of a concrete paving slab. Wear protective gloves, goggles and a face mask.

Level the sand base with a piece of wood

Laying and levelling the slabs

1 Lay five blobs of mortar under each slab

2 Level the slab with a block and hammer

3 Check the fall with a spirit level

4 Fill the joints with a dry mortar mix

Lay the edging slabs on the sand, working in both directions from a corner. When you are satisfied with their positions, lift the slabs one at a time, so you can set them on a bed of mortar (1 part cement : 4 parts sand). Lay a large blob of mortar under each corner, and one more to support the centre of the slab (**1**). If you intend to drive vehicles across the slabs, lay a continuous bed of mortar about 50mm (2in) thick. Wet the back of each slab just before you lay it on top of the mortar. Level each slab by tapping with a heavy hammer, using a block of wood to protect the surface (**2**). Add mortar to fill flush any gaps under the the slabs.

Lay three slabs at a time, inserting spacers between, then check the alignment. To gauge the slope across the paving, drive datum pegs along the high side, with the top of each peg corresponding to the finished surface of the paving, and then use a straightedge with a packing piece under one end to check the fall on the slabs (**3**). Lay the other slabs, each time working outwards from the corner in order to keep the joints square. Remove the spacers before the mortar sets, but don't walk on the paving for 2 to 3 days.

To fill the gaps between the paving slabs, brush a dry mortar mix of 1 part cement : 3 parts sand into the open joints (**4**), then sprinkle the area with a very fine spray of water to consolidate the mortar.

SEE ALSO > Mixing mortar 25, Crossfall 40, Subbase 43

Timber decking

Decking – an offshoot of the American love of outdoor leisure and entertaining – has become extremely popular in this country. Timber is warm to the touch and creates a homely atmosphere that's difficult to achieve with concrete or brick paving. Building a deck can make good use of an area where grass won't grow, or provide a way of covering an unsightly old patio. Being relatively lightweight, wooden decking is ideal for roof gardens, too.

Decking screws
Special plated decking screws are designed to be driven straight into the wood, using a power tool. The longer ones are for building the framework (plated coach screws are a suitable alternative), while the smaller ones are for fixing deck boards to the joists.

Designing your deck

One of the advantages of building in wood is that you can construct a deck to fit a site of almost any shape and size. And you don't have to be a skilled carpenter. However, if you plan to build a raised deck more than 600mm (2ft) from the ground, you should get professional help or advice.

When deciding on the best place for your deck, think about whether you want it to be in the sun most of the time. Or would it be better in a shady spot during the hottest part of the day? It is always worth modifying your design to accommodate trees: just build round them, making sure they have enough room to grow and move with the wind. You may want to take advantage of the view from your garden – but you need to respect your neighbours' privacy, too.

If the best place for your deck is next to the house, incorporate removable panels to gain access to manhole covers and drains – and make sure you don't compromise the damp-proof course or cover airbricks.

Decking materials

Some people like to use reclaimed timber from a salvage yard, or incorporate a variety of materials into their design. However, most of the DIY outlets now stock ready-machined and sanded decking components, which make construction easier.

If you are prepared to pay relatively high prices, you can buy hardwood decking; but softwood is cheaper and perfectly suitable, provided it is tanalized (pressure-treated with preservative) and guaranteed against rot for 15 or 20 years.

Decking materials
Typical components available from DIY outlets:
1 Joists come in various sizes for constructing the underlying framework.
2 Deck boards – plain or ribbed surface.
3 Notched bearer for simple ground-level decks.
4 Newel post for balustrades. The same timber can be used for deck-support posts and corner bracing.
5 Ready-cut stringer for making steps up to a raised deck.
6 Balusters – there's a wide variety of styles.
7 Standard panels or 'tiles' that drop into a framework constructed from notched bearers.
8 Polypropylene sheeting that suppresses weed growth while allowing rainwater to drain away.
9 Fixings – plated decking screws and coach bolts.

Laying ground-level decks

Ground-level decking is simple to construct and ideal for a deck accessed directly from the house. It is also the best option for a roof garden. You can buy factory-made bearers and panels, or make the supporting framework from joists and cover it with smooth or ribbed deck boards.

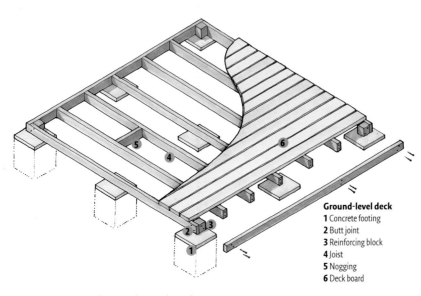

Ground-level deck
1 Concrete footing
2 Butt joint
3 Reinforcing block
4 Joist
5 Nogging
6 Deck board

Bearers and panels

Another method of constructing a ground-level deck is to lay proprietary notched bearers on polypropylene sheeting laid over levelled ground.

If necessary, drive a decking screw into each of the frame joints to make sure the top surfaces of the bearers are flush. Then lay a ready-made panel or deck tile over each square within the framework and secure each panel with decking screws.

Alternatively, cover the framework with deck boards, as described left.

Laying notched bearers
Bearers come with joints already cut to make assembly easier.

Cover the deck bearers with ready-made panels

Constructing the deck

Preparing the ground

Unless you are building onto an existing concrete base, remove any turf and level the ground – ideally adding a shallow layer of gravel topped with sharp sand. Before constructing the deck, lay down a sheet of polypropylene to prevent weed growth.

An even better solution, especially for a garden with poor drainage, is to place your deck on concrete footings (**1**) laid every 1200mm (4ft) across the site. For the footings, dig holes approximately 300mm (1ft) square and 300mm (1ft) deep and fill them with concrete, using a straight beam and a spirit level to check that their top surfaces are all level with one another. Just before the concrete sets hard, shape the exposed edges of the footings with a trowel. For additional protection, place offcuts of bituminous felt (DPC) between the decking and the concrete. Lay polypropylene sheeting between the footings.

Building the framework

Construct the outer frame from joists, butt-jointed at the corners (**2**) and reinforced with blocks cut from 95mm (4in) square posts (**3**). Whenever you cut tanalized timber, you must coat the cut surfaces with a chemical preserver. Screw each joist to the corner blocks, using 80mm (3in) deck-construction

screws. Alternatively, you can use plated coach screws, but will need to drill pilot and clearance holes before inserting them. Whichever you use, stagger the screws to ensure there is sufficient clearance inside the reinforcing block.

Access may be restricted if you are erecting the deck in a corner of the garden – in which case, start by making the internal corner joint first and work outwards from there.

Having constructed the outer frame, cut joists (**4**) to fit snugly inside the frame. Fix them at 400mm (1ft 4in) centres, driving two 145mm (5¾in) deck-construction screws through the framework into each end of every joist; if you are planning to lay the deck boards diagonally, fix the joists at 300mm (1ft) centres. If you can't drive in screws from outside the framework, skew-screw the joists to the frame from the inside using shorter deck-construction screws. Straighten any slightly bowed joists by nailing noggings between them (**5**).

Laying the deck boards

Cut deck boards (**6**) to length and lay them at right angles to the joists. Drive two decking screws through the boards into each joist. Leave a 3 to 6mm (⅛ to ¼in) gap between the boards to provide adequate rainwater runoff.

Fix the first board
Lay the first deck board flush with the frame or allow it to overhang slightly.

Using spacers
As you fix the other boards in place, use a convenient spacer to keep the gaps even.

SEE ALSO > Felt DPC 31, Mixing concrete 39, Concrete mixes 41

Building a raised deck

Support a raised deck on short posts, making allowance for a sloping site. Create interesting changes of level by combining ground-level and raised decks. Don't build a deck higher than 600mm (2ft) without professional help.

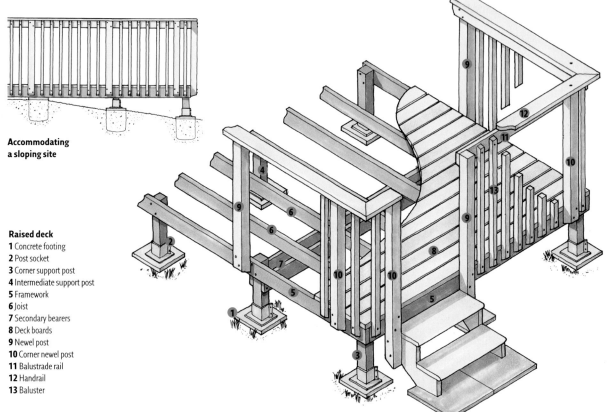

Decking oil
Timber tends to weather naturally to an attractive silver-grey. However, if you want to revive the colour of the wood, coat it with decking oil.

Accommodating a sloping site

Raised deck
1 Concrete footing
2 Post socket
3 Corner support post
4 Intermediate support post
5 Framework
6 Joist
7 Secondary bearers
8 Deck boards
9 Newel post
10 Corner newel post
11 Balustrade rail
12 Handrail
13 Baluster

Constructing the deck

Lay concrete footings (**1**) as for a ground-level deck. Support the deck on 95 x 95mm (4 x 4in) posts, held vertically in metal post sockets (**2**) fixed to each footing with expansion bolts. Support posts are also used to reinforce the outer frame at each corner (**3**) and are placed at 1200mm (4ft) centres across the entire area of the deck (**4**). Construct the outer frame from 140 x 47mm (6 x 2in) joists, screwed to the support posts at each corner (**5**) as for a ground-level deck.

Screw similar-size joists (**6**) between the outer frame members. Fix the joists at 400mm (1ft 4in) centres, driving two 145mm (5¾in) deck-construction screws through the framework into each end of every joist. If you cannot insert the screws from outside the frame, hang the joists from joist hangers attached to the inside of the frame.

Provide additional support for the joists by screwing a pair of 140 x 47mm (6 x 2in) secondary bearers to every second row of support posts (**7**). Fix the deck boards (**8**) in place, as described for a ground-level deck.

Bolt each socket to its footing

Tighten the bolts to clamp the post

Making the balustrade

For safety, every raised deck needs to have a balustrade. Decking manufacturers offer a wide variety of styles. Shown here is a simple balustrade, 1m (3ft 3in) high, constructed from readily available components.

Bolt newel posts, 95 x 95mm (4 x 4in) square, to the outside of the framework (**9**), using two coach bolts per post. Shape the bottom end of each post by cutting a bevel, and saw the top end square. The newel posts should be no more than 1200mm (4ft) apart. Bolt a pair at each corner (**10**), placing each of them 150mm (6in) from the corner of the deck.

Join the newel posts together with a narrow deck board (**11**) screwed to the inside of each row of posts. Butt-joint and screw these rails at the corners.

Screw another deck board to the top edge of the horizontal rail to form a flat handrail (**12**). Mitre the handrails where they meet at the corners, and secure

SEE ALSO > Post sockets 13, Ground-level decks 49

each joint with a single screw driven through the edge.

Screw proprietary balusters (**13**), no more than 100mm (4in) apart, to the horizontal rail and the framework of the deck. Square-section balusters may come with a bevel at each end. If you have to saw the balusters to length, cut a similar bevel to match.

Bolt newel posts to the framework

Building steps

Decking manufacturers supply ready-made components for simple wooden steps. Cut the components to length and screw them together. Then either screw the completed steps to the decking frame-work or, as shown here, bolt the steps to slightly longer newel posts bolted on each side of the steps. Support the base of the steps on levelled paving slabs.

An accumulation of dirt and algae can make the wood slippery. Scrub your deck boards and steps at least once a year with a proprietary decking cleaner.

Adding a skirting

To prevent litter being blown under a raised deck, fit skirting below the framework. You can buy proprietary slatted panels and cut them to fit your deck.

Bolt the steps in place

SEE ALSO > Brick patterns 52

Paving with bricks

Bricks make charming paths. The wide variety of textures and colours available offers endless possibilities of pattern – but choose the type of brick carefully, bearing in mind the sort of use your paving can expect.

Brick paving

Ordinary housebricks are often used for paths and small patios, even though there is the risk of spalling in freezing conditions – unless they happen to be engineering bricks. Their slightly uneven texture and colour are the very reasons why second-hand bricks are so much in demand for garden paving – so a little frost damage is usually acceptable.

However, housebricks are not really suitable if the paved area is to be a parking space or driveway, especially if it's going to be used by heavy vehicles. For a surface that will be durable even under severe conditions, use concrete bricks instead. These are generally slightly smaller than standard housebricks, being something like 200 x 100 x 65mm (8 x 4 x 2½in), but there are many variations in size and also in shape and colour, making possible a wide range of paving – from regular tiled effects to less formal cobbled surfaces.

Brick pavers
Cast-concrete pavers are available in a variety of colours, styles and shapes. Textured setts are ideal for non-slip garden pathways. Brindle concrete blocks are often used for drives and parking areas.

Interlocking concrete pavers

Laying brick paving

Laying bricks over a wide area is very time-consuming, and it helps if at least two people can work together, dividing up the various tasks between them. Also, it's well worth the extra expense of hiring tools that will make the work faster and more efficient.

Brick patterns

Unlike brick walls, which must be bonded in a certain way for stability, brick paths, patios and car-parking areas can be laid to any pattern that appeals to you. Try out your ideas on gridded paper, using the examples shown below for inspiration.

Concrete bricks, which have one finished surface, are often chamfered all round to define their shape and emphasize whatever pattern you choose. Many bricks have spacers moulded into the sides to help form accurate joints. Housebricks can be laid on edge or face down, showing the wide face normally unseen in a wall.

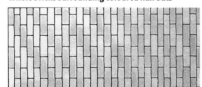
Brick-paved drive and parking space

Herringbone pattern with straight edging

Angled herringbone with straight edging

Whole bricks surrounding coloured half bats

Mottled-brick garden path

Concrete-sett path edged with flush pavers

Providing a base for brick paving

Lay brick pathways and patios on a 75mm (3in) hardcore base, covered with a 50mm (2in) layer of compacted slightly damp sharp sand. When laying concrete bricks for a drive, you need to increase the depth of hardcore to 150mm (6in). Fully compact the hardcore and fill all voids, so that sand from the bedding course is not lost to the sub-base. Provide a crossfall on patios and drives, as for concrete. Make sure that the surface of the paving is not less than 150mm (6in) below a DPC protecting a building.

Retaining edges

Unless the brick path is laid against a wall or some similar structure, the edges of the paving must be contained by a permanent restraint. Timber treated with chemical preserver is one solution, constructed like the formwork for concrete. The edging boards should be flush with the surface of the path, but drive the stakes below ground so that they can be covered by soil or turf.

Concrete paving, in particular, needs a more substantial edging of bricks set in concrete. Dig a trench that is deep and wide enough to take a row of bricks on end plus a 100mm (4in) concrete 'foundation'. Lay the bricks while the concrete is still wet – holding them in place temporarily with a staked board while you pack more concrete behind the edging. Once the concrete has set, remove the board and lay hardcore and sand in the excavation.

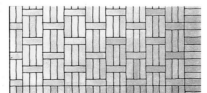
Stretcher-bond brickwork

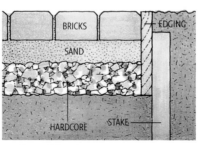
Wooden retaining edge

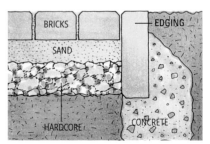
Brick retaining edge

Cane-weave pattern

SEE ALSO > Engineering bricks 21, Brick bonding 26, Mixing concrete 39, Fall for patios and drives 40, Erecting formwork 42, Laying hardcore 43

Compacting and levelling the sand

When the bricks are first laid on the sand they should project 10mm (³⁄₈in) above the edging restraints, to allow for bedding them in at a later stage.

Spread sand to about two-thirds of its finished thickness across the area to be paved and then compact it, using a hired vibrating plate.

Spread more sand on top and level it with a notched spreader that spans the edging (1).

If the paving is too wide for a spreader, lay levelling battens on the hardcore base and scrape the sand to the required depth using a straightedge (2). Then remove the battens and fill the voids carefully with sand.

Vibrating plate
Use a petrol-driven vibrating plate for levelling and bedding in concrete pavers.

1 Level the sand with a notched spreader

2 Or lay levelling battens on the hardcore

Bedding in the bricks

Lay the bricks on the sand to your chosen pattern. Work from one end of the site, kneeling on a board placed across the bricks (3). Never stand on the bed of sand. Lay whole bricks only, leaving any gaps at the edges to be filled with cut bricks after you have laid an area of approximately 1 to 2sq m (1 to 2½sq yd). Concrete bricks have fixed spacers, so butt them together tightly.

Fill any of the remaining spaces with bricks cut with a bolster and club hammer. If you are paving a large area, it's worth hiring a purpose-made guillotine.

When the area of paving is complete, run the vibrating plate over the surface two or three times, until it has worked the bricks down into the sand and flush with the outer edging (4).

Vibrating the bricks will work some sand up between them; complete the job by brushing more kiln-dried joint-filling sand across the finished paving and vibrating it into the open joints.

Brick guillotine
Hire a guillotine to cut concrete paving bricks.

3 Lay the bricks to your chosen pattern

4 A vibrating plate levels brick paving perfectly

SEE ALSO > Cutting bricks 28

Drainage accessories

An existing manhole cover often spoils the appearance of paving. The solution is to replace the cover with a special hollow version that is designed to be filled with concrete bricks and merges into the surrounding paving.

Draining rainwater from a large flat area of paving can be a problem. One solution is to include one or more linear drainage channels running to a soakaway.

Manhole cover

Inset manhole cover
The metal frame of an inset manhole cover should be bedded in concrete, which is then overlaid with paving that runs right up to the rim of the access hole. Make sure the rim is just below the finished surface of the paving.

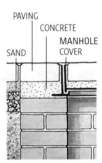

Frame bedded in concrete

Linear drainage channel
Plastic U-section drainage channels linked end to end are bedded in a 100mm (4in) concrete base, which is haunched (built up on both sides) to hold the channel in place. The first row of bricks on each side of the channel is bedded in the concrete, and should finish 3 to 6mm (⅛ to ¼in) above the level of the plastic or metal grating used to cover the channel.

A special end cap is available for connecting to a main drain, or you can drain the water into a soakaway about 1m (4ft) square and at least 1m (4ft) deep. Fill the soakaway with coarse rubble, up to the level of the hardcore base laid for the paving.

Cutting the channel
Use a panel saw to cut a plastic drainage channel to length.

Building garden steps

Designing a garden for a sloping site offers plenty of possibilities for creating attractive changes of level – by terracing areas of paving or having planting beds held in place by retaining walls. However, so people are able to move from one level to another safely, at least one flight of steps will be required.

Designing steps

If you have a large garden where the slope is very gradual, a series of steps with wide treads and low risers can make an impressive feature.

If the slope is steep, to avoid a staircase appearance construct a flight of steps composed of a few treads interposed with wide flat landings – where the flight can change direction to add further interest and offer a different view of the garden. In fact, a shallow flight can be virtually a series of landings, perhaps circular in plan, sweeping up the slope in a curve.

For steps to be both comfortable and safe to use, the proportion of tread (the part you stand on) to riser (the vertical part of the step) is important. As a rough guide, construct steps so that the depth of the tread (from front to back) plus twice the height of the riser equals 650mm (2ft 2in). For example, match 300mm (1ft) treads with 175mm (7in) risers; 350mm (1ft 2in) treads with 150mm (6in) risers; and so on. Never make treads less than 300mm (1ft) deep, or risers higher than 175mm (7in).

● **Slippery steps**
Steps can become slippery if algae is allowed to grow on the treads. Brush affected steps with a solution of 1 part household bleach to 4 parts water. After 48 hours, wash them with clean water and repeat the treatment. You can also treat the steps with a proprietary fungicidal solution.

Paved steps built with natural-stone risers

Using concrete slabs

Paving slabs in their various forms are ideal for making firm, flat treads for garden steps. Construct the risers from concrete blocks or bricks, allowing the treads to overhang by 25 to 50mm (1 to 2in) in order to cast a shadow line to define the edge of the step.

So you can gauge the number of steps required, measure the difference in height from the top of the slope to the bottom. Next, mark the position of the risers with pegs and roughly shape the steps in the soil.

Either lay concrete slabs, bedded in sand, flush with the ground at the foot of the slope or dig a trench for hardcore and a 100 to 150mm (4 to 6in) concrete base to support the first riser (**1**). When the concrete has set, construct the riser from two courses of mortared bricks, checking the alignment with a spirit level (**2**). Fill behind the riser with compacted hardcore until it is level, then lay the tread on a bed of mortar (**3**). Using a spirit level as a guide, tap down the tread until it slopes very slightly towards its front edge, in order to shed rainwater and so prevent ice forming.

Measure from the front edge of the tread to mark the position of the next riser on the slabs (**4**), then construct the next step in the same way.

Landscaping each side
It is usually possible to landscape the slope at each side of a flight of steps and to turf or plant it to prevent the soil washing down onto the steps. Another solution is to retain the soil with large stones, perhaps extending into a rockery on one or both sides.

1 Dig the footing for the first riser

2 Build a brick riser and level it

3 Lay the tread on mortar

4 Mark the position of the next riser

Paving-slab steps
A section through a simple flight of garden steps built with brick risers and paving slabs.
1 Concrete footing
2 Brick-built riser
3 Hardcore infill
4 Paving-slab tread

SEE ALSO > Mixing mortar 25; Footings 27, Bricklaying techniques 28, Retaining walls 36, Paving slabs 46

Repairing concrete steps

Casting new steps in concrete requires such complicated formwork that the end result hardly justifies the effort involved, especially when it's possible to construct better-looking steps from cast-concrete slabs and blocks. Nevertheless, if you have a flight of concrete steps in your garden, you will want to keep them in good condition.

Like other forms of masonry, concrete suffers from 'spalling' – frost breaks down the surface of the material and fragments flake off. Spalling frequently occurs along the front edges of steps where foot traffic adds to the problem. Repair broken edges as soon as you can – since, as well as being unattractive, damaged steps can be dangerous.

Building up broken edges

Wearing safety goggles, chip away some of the concrete around the damaged area to provide a good grip for fresh concrete. Cut a board to the height of the riser and prop it against the step (**1**).

Mix a small batch of general-purpose concrete, adding a little PVA bonding agent to help it adhere to the step. Dilute some bonding agent with water (say, 3 parts water : 1 part bonding agent) and brush it onto the damaged area, stippling it into the crevices. When the surface becomes tacky, fill the hole with concrete mix flush with the edge of the board (**2**). Radius the front edge slightly with an edging float, running it against the board.

1 Prop a board against the riser

2 Fill the front edge with concrete

Building log steps

You can use sawn lengths of timber to build attractive steps that suit an informal garden. As it's not always possible to obtain uniform logs, you may have to make up the height of the riser with two or more slimmer logs. Alternatively, buy purpose-made pressure-treated logs, machined with a flat surface on two faces. Soak your own timber in chemical preserver.

Remove any turf and cut a regular slope in the earth bank, then compact the soil by treading it down. Sharpen stakes cut from logs 75mm (3in) in diameter and drive them into the ground, one at each end of a step (**1**).

Place a heavy log behind the stakes, bedding it down in the soil until it is level (**2**), and pack broken-brick hardcore behind it to construct the tread of the step (**3**). To finish the step, shovel a layer of gravel on top of the hardcore, then rake the gravel level with the top of the log riser.

If you're unable to obtain large logs, you can build a step from two or three straight slimmer logs, holding them against the stakes with hardcore as you construct the riser (**4**).

Finish by laying a gravel path at the top and bottom of the flight of steps.

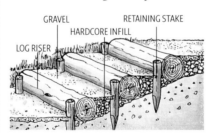

GRAVEL   RETAINING STAKE
HARDCORE INFILL
LOG RISER

Log steps

Making curved steps

To build a series of curved steps, choose materials that will make construction as easy as possible. One option is to use tapered concrete slabs for the treads, designing the circumference of the steps to suit the proportions of the slabs. Alternatively, use bricks laid flat or on edge to build the risers. Set the bricks to radiate from the centre of the curve, and fill the slightly tapered joints with mortar. Use a length of string attached to a peg driven into the ground as an improvised compass to mark out the curve of each step.

After roughly shaping the soil, lay a concrete foundation for the bottom riser. Build the risers and treads as for regular paving-slab steps (see opposite), using the improvised string compass as a guide.

1 Drive a stake at each end of a step

2 Place a log behind the stakes

3 Fill behind the log with hardcore

4 Make up a riser with two slim logs

Log steps

Paved circular landing

Curved steps made entirely from bricks

SEE ALSO > Footings 27, Concrete mixes 41, Edging float 43, Laying hardcore 43, Tapered slabs 46

Creating water gardens

There is nothing like still or running water to enliven a garden. Waterfalls and fountains have an almost mesmerizing fascination, and the sound of trickling water has a delightfully soothing effect. Even a small area of still water will support all manner of interesting pond life and plants – with the additional bonus of the images of trees, rocks and sky reflected in its placid surface.

Well worth it
A healthy pond requires careful construction to begin with and regular maintenance thereafter. However, the effort will be amply repaid – especially if you include some form of running water to add sound and sparkling light to the scene.

SEE ALSO > Installing pond liners 58–9, Building a cascade 61

Pond liners

It's not by chance that the number of garden ponds has greatly increased in recent years. Their popularity is largely due to the fact that easily installed rigid and flexible pond liners are now readily available, which make it possible to create a water garden by putting in just a few days' work.

In the past it was necessary to line a pond with concrete. While it is true that concrete is a very versatile material, there is always the possibility of a leak developing through cracks caused by ground movement or the force of expanding ice. There are no such worries with flexible liners or those made from rigid plastic. Building formers for a concrete pond involves both labour and expense, and when the pond is finished it has to be left to season for about a month – during which time it needs to be emptied and refilled a number of times to ensure that the water will be safe for fish and plant life. In contrast, you can introduce plants into a pool lined with plastic or rubber as soon as the water itself has matured, which takes no more than a few days.

Ordering a flexible liner

Use a simple formula to calculate the size of the liner you will need. Disregarding any complicated shapes and planting shelves and so on, simply take the overall length and width of the pond and add twice the maximum depth to each dimension to arrive at the size of the liner. If possible, adapt your design to fall within the nearest stock liner size – or you will have to pay extra for a special order.

POND DIMENSIONS	
Length – 3m	9ft 9in
Width – 2m	6ft 6in
Depth – 450mm	1ft 6in
SIZE OF LINER	
3m + 0.900m = 3.9m	9ft 9in + 3ft = 12ft 9in
2m + 0.900m = 2.9m	6ft 6in + 3ft = 9ft 6in

Choosing a pond liner

The advantages of proprietary pond liners over concrete are fairly obvious, but there are a number of options to choose from – depending on the size and shape of the pond you wish to create and how much you are planning to spend.

Pond under construction
This ambitious project uses a flexible liner in the construction of a water garden.

Rigid plastic liners
Regular visitors to garden centres will be familiar with the range of preformed plastic pond liners. A rigid liner is in effect a ready-made one-piece pond – including planting shelves and, in some cases, recessed troughs to accommodate marsh or bog gardens.

The best pond liners are those made from rigid glass-reinforced plastic (fibreglass), which is very strong and is also resistant to the effects of frost or ice. Almost as good – and more economical – are liners made from vacuum-formed plastic. Provided they are handled with a reasonable degree of care and installed correctly, rigid plastic pond liners are practically leak-proof. A very acceptable water garden can be created with a carefully selected series of pond liners linked together by watercourses.

Flexible liners
For complete freedom of design, choose a flexible-sheet liner that will hug the contours of a pond of virtually any shape and size.

For a relatively inexpensive flexible pond liner, choose a polyvinyl acetate (PVC) sheet in the region of 0.35 mm thick. More durable PVC liners are available in thicknesses of about 0.5mm. Plastic liners are guaranteed for many years of normal use – but if you want your pond to last for 50 years or more, choose a thicker membrane made from synthetic rubber.

Black rubber liners are made in a wide range of stock sizes, up to about 10 x 15m (32 x 50ft). The thicker the liner, the more likely it is to crease as you fill the pond with water. However, creases are hardly noticeable once the pond has matured.

Rigid pond liner
Rigid liners are moulded from plastic.

Flexible liner
The best-quality flexible liners are made from butyl.

SEE ALSO > Installing pond liners 58–9, Building a cascade 61

Constructing ponds

A pond must be sited correctly if it is to have any chance of maturing into an attractive, clear stretch of water. Don't place a pond under deciduous trees: falling leaves will pollute the water as they decay, causing fish to become ill or die. Laburnum trees are especially poisonous.

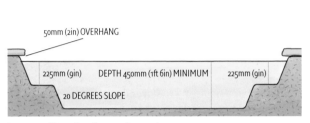

Important dimensions for a garden pond

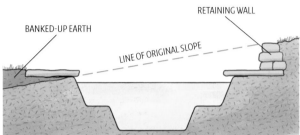

Accommodating a sloping site

The need for sunlight
Although sunlight promotes the growth of algae – which causes ponds to turn a pea-green colour – it is also necessary to encourage the growth of water plants. An abundance of oxygenating plants will compete with the algae for mineral salts and, aided by the shade that is cast by floating and marginal plants, they will help to keep the water clear.

Volume of water
The pond's dimensions are important in creating harmony between plants and fish. It is difficult to maintain the right conditions for clear water in a pond that is less than 3.75sq m (40sq ft) in surface area – but the volume of water is even more vital. A pond up to about 9sq m (100sq ft) in area needs to be 450mm (1ft 6in) deep. As the area increases you will have to dig deeper, to about 600mm (2ft) or more, although it's hardly ever necessary to dig deeper than 750mm (2ft 6in).

Designing the shape of your pond
Although there's a huge variety of rigid plastic liners available, you are limited to the shapes selected by the manufacturers. There are no such limitations if you use a flexible pond liner, although curved shapes take up the slack better than straight-sided pools do.

The profile of the pond must be designed to fulfil certain requirements. To grow marginal plants, you will need a shelf 225mm (9in) wide around the edge of the pond, 225mm (9in) below the surface of the water. This will take a standard 150mm (6in) planting crate, with ample water above, and you can always raise the crate on bricks or pieces of paving. The sides of the pond should slope at about 20 degrees, to prevent the collapse of soil during construction and to allow the liner to stretch without promoting too many creases. It will also allow a sheet of ice to float upwards without damaging the liner. Judge the angle by measuring 75mm (3in) inwards for every 225mm (9in) of depth. If the soil is very sandy, increase the angle of slope slightly.

Installing a rigid liner

Stand a rigid pond liner in position and prop it up with cardboard boxes, both to check its orientation and to mark its perimeter on the ground.

Use a spirit level to plot key points on the ground (**1**) and mark them with small pegs. You will need to dig outside this line, so absolute accuracy is not required.

Lay a straightedge across the top and measure the depth of the excavation (**2**), including marginal shelves. Keep the excavation as close as possible to the shape of the liner, but extend it by 150mm (6in) on all sides. Compact the base and cover it with a layer of sharp sand 25mm (1in) deep. Lower the liner and bed it down firmly into the sand. Check that the pool stands level (**3**) and wedge it temporarily but firmly with wooden battens until the backfill of soil or sand can hold it.

Start to fill the liner with water from a hose and, at the same time, pour sifted soil or dry sand behind the liner (**4**). There's no need to hurry, as it will take some time to fill the pond. Reach into the excavation and pack soil under the marginal shelves with your hands.

When the liner is firmly bedded in the soil, either finish the edge with stones as for a flexible liner (see opposite) or re-lay turf to cover the rim of the liner.

1 Mark the perimeter of the liner

2 Measure the depth of the excavation

3 Make sure the liner stands level

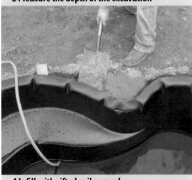

4 Infill with sifted soil or sand

SEE ALSO > Rigid liners 57, Building a rockery 61

Installing a flexible liner

Mark out the shape of the pond on the ground – a garden hose is useful for trying out curves. Before you start excavating the soil, look down from an upstairs window at the shape you have plotted, to make sure you are happy with the proportions of your pond.

Excavating and lining the pond

Excavate the pond to the level of the planting shelf, then mark and dig out the deeper sections (**1**). Remove sharp stones and roots from the sides and bottom of the excavation.

The slabs surrounding the pond need to be 18mm (¾in) below the turf. Cut back the turf to allow for the stones, and then every metre (3ft) or so drive wooden datum pegs into the exposed surround. Level the tops of all the pegs, and use a straightedge (**2**) to check the level across the pond as well. Remove or pack earth around the pegs to bring the surrounding soil to a consistent level.

When the surround is level, remove the pegs and, to cushion the liner, spread a 12 to 25mm (½ to 1in) layer of slightly damp sand over the base and sides of the excavation (**3**). Alternatively, cover the excavation with a proprietary pond-liner underlay.

Installing the liner
Drape the liner across the excavation with an even overlap all round. Hold it in place with bricks while you introduce water from a hose (**4**). Filling a large pond will take several hours, but check the liner regularly, moving the bricks as it stretches. A few creases are inevitable, but you can lose most of them if you keep the liner fairly taut and ease it into shape as the water rises.

When the level reaches 50mm (2in) below the edge of the liner, turn off the water. Cut off surplus liner with scissors, leaving a 150mm (6in) overlap all round (**5**). Push long nails through the overlap into the soil, so the liner can't slip.

Laying the surround
Select flat stones that follow the shape of the pond, with a reasonably close fit between them. Let the stones project over the water by about 50mm (2in).

Wearing goggles, use a bolster chisel to cut stones to fit the gaps behind the larger edging stones. Lift the stones one or two at a time and bed them on two or three strategically placed mounds of mortar, composed of 1 part cement : 3 parts soft sand (**6**).

Tap the stones level with a mallet and fill the joints with a trowel – use a paintbrush to smooth the joints. Don't drop mortar into the water, or you will have to refill the pond before introducing fish or plants.

Stopping your pond overflowing

Every garden pond needs topping up from time to time – and, as many gardeners know to their cost, it is all too easy to forget to turn off the water and flood the garden when the pond overflows. As a precaution, build a simple drain beneath the pond's edging stones to allow excess water to escape. This also provides a means of running electric flex into the pond to power a pump or lighting.

Cut corrugated-plastic sheet to make two strips, about 150mm (6in) wide and long enough to run under the edging stones. Pop-rivet the strips together to make a channel about 25mm (1in) deep.

Scrape earth and sand from beneath the liner to make a shallow recess that will accommodate the channel laid on top of the liner; then lay edging stones on top to hold the channel in place. Dig a small soakaway behind the channel and fill it up to the level of the stones with rubble topped with turf or fine gravel.

Drain components   **Place the drain beneath the edging stones**

1 Dig the excavation as accurately as possible

2 Level the edge using datum pegs

3 Line the excavation with damp sand

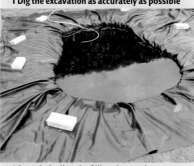
4 Stretch the liner by filling the pond

5 Cut the flexible liner to fit

6 Lay edging stones to complete the pond

SEE ALSO > Cutting slabs 47, Flexible liners 57, Pumps 60

Raised-edged ponds

If you want a more formal pond, you can build a raised edge using bricks or concrete blocks. A surround about 450mm (1ft 6in) high serves as a deterrent for small children while also providing seating. If you prefer a lower wall, say 225mm (9in) high, create planting shelves at ground level, digging the pond deeper in the centre. Place planting crates on blocks around the edge of a deep raised pond.

Building the edging

Lay 100 to 150mm (4 to 6in) concrete footings to support walls constructed from two skins of masonry set apart to match the width of flat coping stones. Allow for an overhang of 50mm (2in) over the water's edge, and lap the outer wall by 12 to 18mm (½ to ¾in). To save money, you may prefer to use cheap common bricks or plain concrete blocks for the inner skin, while reserving more expensive decorative bricks or facing blocks for the outer skin of the wall.

You can either line a raised pond with a standard flexible liner or order a prefabricated fitted liner to reduce the amount of creasing at the corners. Trap the edge of the liner underneath the coping stones.

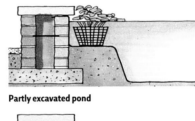

Partly excavated pond

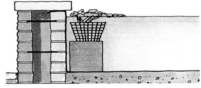

Fully raised pond built with a cavity wall

Raised-edge pond
A beautifully designed water feature, built from artificial-stone blocks and coping slabs. The small cascade is powered by a submersible pump.

Alternative pond edging

An edging of flat stones is useful for tending water plants and fish, but often a more natural setting is required. Incorporate a shelf around the pond – as for marginal plants, though this time it is for an edging of rocks. If you place them carefully, there is no need to mortar them in. Arrange rocks behind the edging to cover the liner.

In order to create a shallow beach-like edging, slope the soil at a very shallow angle and lay large pebbles or flat rocks upon the liner. You can merge them with a rockery, or let them form a natural water line.

To discourage cats poaching fish from the pond, create an edging of trailing plants – without a firm foothold, a cat will feel uncomfortable reaching into water. Bed a strip of soft wire netting in the mortar below the edging stones, and cut the strip to over-hang the water by about 150mm (6in) as a support for the plants. Once established, the plants, will disguise the edge of the liner.

Rock-edged pond

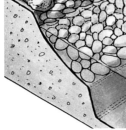

Pebble-strewn shelf

A wire edge supports plants

Pumps and fountains

Submersible pumps for fountains and cascades are operated either directly from the mains electrical supply or via a transformer that reduces the voltage. Get a qualified electrician to help you install the necessary equipment.

An extra-low-voltage pump is perfectly safe, and can be installed and wired simply. Place the pump in the water and run its cable beneath the edging stones, to a waterproof connector attached to the extension lead of a transformer installed inside the house. With this system, you can remove the pump for servicing without disturbing the extension cable or transformer. Run the pump regularly, to keep it in good working order.

Place a submersible cascade pump close to the edge of the pond, so that you can disconnect the hose running to the cascade when you need to service the pump. Stand a fountain unit on a flat stone, so the jet of water is vertical. Plant water lilies some distance away from a fountain, as falling water will encourage the flowers to close up.

Combination pump and filter
For efficient filtration of the pond water, install a separate filter tank, which you can bury beside the pond or hide with planting (see opposite). However, for small ponds with low fish stocks, you can buy a submersible pump with its own built-in filtration system and ultra-violet clarifier that will prevent the water turning green due to the presence of algae. Some units include a fountain head and an outlet to deliver water to a cascade.

SEE ALSO > Choosing bricks 21–2, Concrete blocks 23, Footings 27, Laying bricks 28–33, Flexible liners 57

Building a rockery and cascade

A cascade running through a tastefully planted rockery adds a further dimension to a water garden. The technique for building a series of watercourses is not as complicated as you might expect – and at the same time you can cover much of the groundwork needed to create the rockery. Providing running water is also an ideal way of filtering your pond.

You will be surprised at the amount of soil produced by excavating a pond. To avoid waste and the trouble of transporting it to a local dump, use it to create a poolside rockery. If you include a filter and a small reservoir on the higher ground, you can pump water from the main pond through the filter into the reservoir and return it via the trickling cascade.

If you order them from a garden centre, buying a large enough number of natural stones to give the impression of a real rocky outcrop can work out extremely expensive. A cheaper way is to use cast reproduction rocks, which will eventually weather in quite well. However, your best option is to purchase natural stone direct from a local quarry. Rocks can be very heavy, so get the quarry to deliver as close to the site as possible; and hire a strong trolley to move individual stones about the garden.

A rockery and cascade are built as one operation, but for the sake of clarity they are described separately here.

Lifting large stones
Use a rope to lift and position large rocks.

Creating a cascade

Rigid-liner manufacturers make moulded cascade kits for embedding in rockeries – you simply cover the edges with stones, soil and trailing plants. Alternatively, you may prefer to create your own custom-made watercourse, using offcuts of flexible liner.

Installing the liner
So that the cascade can discharge directly into the main pond, form a small inlet at the side of the pond by leaving a large flap of flexible liner (**1**). Build shallow banks at each side of the inlet and line it with stones. Create a stepped watercourse ascending in stages to the reservoir. Line the watercourse with flexible liner, over-lapping the offcuts on the face of each cascade. Tuck the edge of each lower piece of liner under the edge of the piece above, and hold the pieces in place with stones.

To retain water in small pools along the watercourse, cut each step with a slope towards the rear (**2**) and place stones along the lip for the desired effect (**3**). A flat stone will produce a sheet of water; a layer of pebbles will create a rippling cascade. As the construction work progresses, test the watercourse by running water from a garden hose.

Bury the flexible hose from the cascade pump in the rockery – making sure there are no sharp bends, which would restrict the flow of water. Attach the hose to the filter tank at the top of the watercourse (**4**). Conceal the tank behind rocks at the back of the rockery, where it can discharge filtered water into the reservoir.

A rigid plastic reservoir will have a lip moulded in one edge, which allows water to escape down the watercourse. If you use flexible liner to construct a reservoir (**5**), you will need to shape the edge to form a low point (**6**) and support a flat stone over the opening in order to hide the liner.

Filter tanks
Pumps usually have built-in foam filters, but these are not sufficient to keep the water in a sizeable pond clear and healthy enough for fish. It is preferable to install a plastic tank containing a combination of foam filters that will remove debris, plus a layer of biological filter medium to take out pollutants created by rotting vegetation and fish excreta.

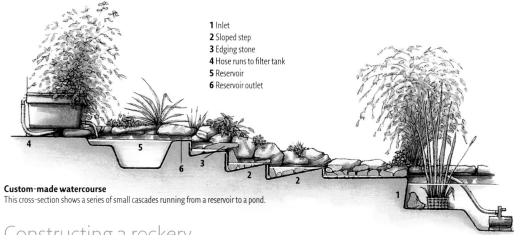

1 Inlet
2 Sloped step
3 Edging stone
4 Hose runs to filter tank
5 Reservoir
6 Reservoir outlet

Custom-made watercourse
This cross-section shows a series of small cascades running from a reservoir to a pond.

Constructing a rockery

To create an illusion of layers of rock, select and place each stone in a rockery carefully. Stones placed haphazardly at odd angles tend to resemble a spoil heap rather than a natural outcrop. Take care not to strain yourself when lifting rocks. Keep your feet together and use your leg muscles to do the work, keeping your back as straight as possible. To move a particularly heavy rock, slip a rope around it.

Lay large flat rocks to form the front edge of the rockery, placing soil behind and between them to form a level platform. Compact the soil to anchor the rocks.

Lay subsequent layers of rock set back from the first, but not in a regular pattern. Place some to create steep embankments, others to form a gradual slope of wide steps. As the work progresses, brush soil off the rocks into the crevices.

SEE ALSO > Pond liners 57

Creating a pebble pool

One of the pleasures of a secluded garden is to be able to appreciate the sounds of birdsong and rustling trees and the rippling tones of running water. Given the right location, nature provides the wind and the birds – but in most cases we have to supply the running water ourselves.

Given sufficient space, most people opt for a fountain or a small cascade trickling into a garden pond. But what if you only have a small garden or patio? A space-saving water feature is the ideal solution. All you need is a submersible recirculating pump placed in a miniature moulded-plastic pool set in the ground and covered with decorative pebbles. This type of water feature can be situated close to the house – within earshot of the windows and conveniently placed for wiring into your power supply.

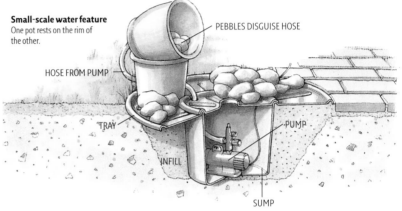

Small-scale water feature
One pot rests on the rim of the other.

PEBBLES DISGUISE HOSE
HOSE FROM PUMP
TRAY
PUMP
INFILL
SUMP

Installing a moulded pool

Moulded-plastic pools take the form of shallow round or square trays with a deep bucket-like centre section or sump. A perforated or moulded lid is provided to cover the sump and to support the layer of pebbles that are used to disguise the feature once it has been installed.

Excavating the pool
Start by digging a hole slightly larger than the size of the tray. Make the hole deep enough to set the edge of the tray level with or just below the surface of the patio. You also need to allow for a layer of sand – to be placed on the compacted base of the excavated hole – on which to bed the sump. Set the sump in place and partially fill it with water to help keep it steady. Carefully backfill the sides with earth or sand; build up the infill until the sump and tray are well supported and level.

Fitting the pump
Following the manufacturer's instructions, connect the pump's cable to your power supply – which must include a residual current device (RCD), in order to protect the circuit. Ask an electrician to help with the installation.

Drill a discreet hole in a convenient door or window frame for the pump's cable, and seal the gap around the cable with silicone sealant.

Connect a length of hose to the pump's water outlet and then place the pump in the sump, which you can now fill with water. Test that the pump is working. Lead the hose to one side and fit the lid in place. It may be necessary to trim the edge of the lid in order to accommodate the hose.

Making the cascade
Two ceramic plant pots can make a simple cascade. Balance one of the pots at an angle on the rim of the other one and stand them on the tray. Feed the end of the hose into the drain hole in the bottom of the angled pot and then seal the hole with silicone sealant. You may find this is easier to do if you disconnect the hose from the pump once the hose has been cut to length.

With the pots in position, place some random-size pebbles around them to cover the sump tray. Put a few pebbles inside the angled pot, to weigh it down and conceal the end of the hose. Arrange potted plants to help disguise the hose at the rear. Run the pump, and try various arrangements of pebbles in and around the pots to create an attractive surround.

Routine maintenance

Top up the buried sump occasionally to make up for natural evaporation.

At the end of the season, remove the pump and clean the filter. This will mean rearranging the pebbles, which provides an opportunity to remove leaf litter and to clean up generally.

● **Water-feature pump**
For a patio water feature, choose a small cascade-type pump. If you're in doubt about the performance of a particular unit, check the manufacturer's literature or, if need be, consult your supplier.

SEE ALSO > Pumps and fountains 60

Reference

Reference

Building tools

A specialist such as a plasterer, joiner or bricklayer needs only a limited set of tools, whereas the amateur is more like a one-man general builder – who has to be able to tackle all kinds of construction and repair work and therefore requires a much wider range of tools. The tool kit suggested here is for making repairs and improvements to your home and for tasks such as erecting garden structures and laying paving.

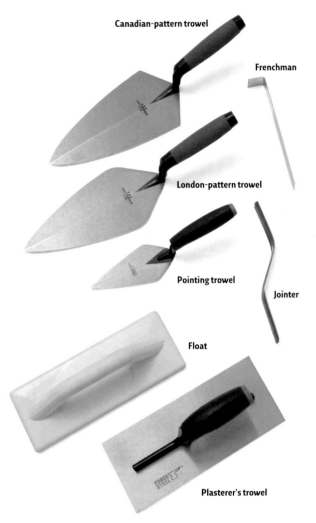

Canadian-pattern trowel

Frenchman

London-pattern trowel

Pointing trowel

Jointer

Float

Plasterer's trowel

Floats and trowels

For a professional builder, floats and trowels have their specific uses – but in home maintenance a repointing trowel may often be the ideal tool for patching small areas of plaster, or a plasterer's trowel for smoothing concrete.

Brick trowels

A brick trowel is for handling and placing mortar when laying bricks or concrete blocks. A professional might use one with a blade as long as 300mm (1ft) – but such a trowel is too heavy and unwieldy for the amateur, so buy a good-quality brick trowel with a fairly short blade.

The blade of a London-pattern trowel has one curved edge for cutting bricks, a skill that takes practice to perfect. The blade's other edge is straight, for picking up mortar. You can buy left-handed versions of this trowel, or opt for a similar trowel with two straight edges.

A Canadian-pattern trowel (sometimes called a Philadelphia brick trowel) is also symmetrical, having a wide blade with two curved edges.

Pointing trowel

A pointing trowel is designed for repairing and shaping mortar joints between bricks. The blade is only about 100mm (4in) long.

Jointer

Use a jointer to shape concave mortar joints between bricks. The tool's narrow blade is dragged along the horizontal and vertical joints, shaping the mortar into shallow depressions.

Frenchman

A Frenchman is a specialized tool for scraping off excess mortar from brick-work jointing. You can make one by heating and bending an old table knife or a metal strip.

Wooden or plastic float

A wooden builder's float is for applying and smoothing cement renderings and concrete to a fine, attractive texture. The more expensive ones have detachable handles, so their wooden blades can be replaced when they wear. Similar floats made from plastic are also available.

Plasterer's trowel

A plasterer's trowel is a steel float for applying plaster and cement renderings to walls. Dampened, it is also used for 'polishing' – smoothing the surface of the material when it has firmed up. Some builders prefer to apply rendering with a heavy trowel and finish it with a more flexible blade, but you need to be quite skilled to exploit such subtle differences.

Boards for carrying mortar or plaster

Any convenient-sized sheet of 12 or 18mm (½ or ¾in) exterior-grade plywood can be used as a mixing board for plaster or mortar. A panel about 1m (3ft) square makes an ideal mixing board, while a smaller spot board, about 600mm (2ft) square, is convenient for carrying the material to the work site. Screw some battens to the underside of either board to make it easier to lift and carry. You will also need a lightweight hawk for carrying pointing mortar or plaster.

A home-made hawk
Make a hawk by nailing a block of wood underneath a plywood board, so you can plug a handle into it.

Using a pointing hawk
A pointing hawk makes the filling of mortar joints very easy. Place the lip of the hawk just under a horizontal joint and scrape the mortar into place with a small trowel or jointer.

SEE ALSO > Mortar 25, Bricklaying 28–33

Tools for levelling and measuring

Tape measure
An ordinary retractable steel tape measure is adequate for most purposes. But if you need to measure a large plot, buy or hire a wind-up tape, which can be up to 30m (100ft) in length.

Builder's square
A large set square is useful when setting out brick or concrete-block corners. The best squares are stamped out of sheet metal, but you can make a serviceable one by cutting out a right-angled triangle from thick plywood with a hypotenuse of about 750mm (2ft 6in). Cut out the centre of the triangle to reduce the weight.

Spirit level
A spirit level is a machine-made straightedge incorporating special glass tubes or vials that contain a liquid. In each vial an air bubble floats. When a bubble rests exactly between two lines marked on the glass, that indicates that the structure on which the level is held is properly horizontal or vertical, depending on the orientation of the vial.

Buy a wooden or lightweight aluminium level 600 to 900mm (2 to 3ft) long. A well-made one is very strong, but treat it with care and always clean mortar or plaster from it before they set.

Try square
Use a large try square for marking out square cuts or joints on timber. The same tool is used to check that wood is planed square and to make sure an internal corner forms a right angle.

Plumb line
A small, heavy weight hung on a length of fine string is used for judging whether a structure or surface is vertical.

Bricklayer's line
This is a nylon line used as a guide for laying bricks or blocks level. It is stretched between two flat-bladed pins – which are driven into vertical joints at the ends of a wall – or between line blocks that hook over the bricks at the ends of a course. As a substitute, you can stretch string between two stakes driven into the ground outside the line of the wall.

Steel pins and line
You can buy special flat-bladed pins, or make your own by hammering flats on 100mm (4in) nails.

Line blocks
The blocks grip the corners of the bricks at the end of a course, and the line passes through their slots.

Plasterer's rule
This is simply a straight length of wood that is used for scraping plaster and rendering undercoats level.

Straightedge
Any length of straight rigid timber can be used to check whether a surface is flat or, in conjunction with a spirit level, to see whether two points are at the same height.

Gauge stick
For gauging the height of brick courses, calibrate a softwood batten by making sawcuts across it at 75mm (3in) intervals – which is the thickness of a brick plus its mortar joint.

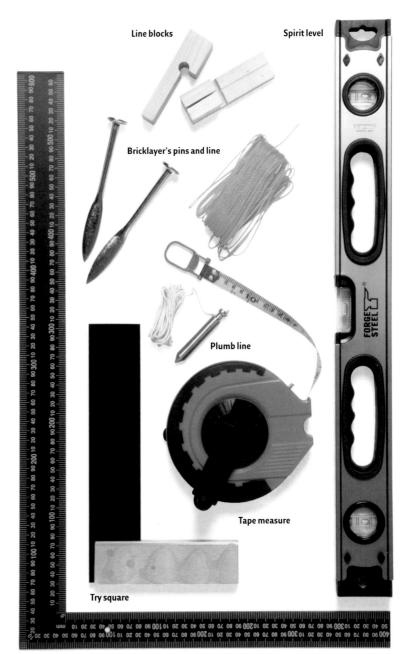

Line blocks

Spirit level

Bricklayer's pins and line

Plumb line

Tape measure

Try square

Builder's square

Using a water level

A water level comprises a flexible hose full of water with a short transparent gauge at each end. Since water level remains constant, the levels in the gauges are always identical and so can be used for marking identical heights, even over long distances and round obstacles and bends.

If you don't want to buy a water level, make one by plugging short lengths of transparent plastic tubing into the ends of a garden hose. Then fill the hose with water until it appears in both tubes.

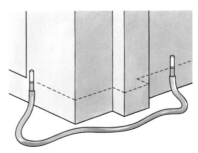

Measuring around a corner
One distinct advantage of using a water level is being able to take measurements around a corner.

SEE ALSO ▸ Bricklaying 28–33

Hammers

Several types of hammer are useful on a building site.

Claw hammer

Choose a strong claw hammer for building stud partitions, making doorframes and window frames, nailing floorboards and putting up garden fencing.

Club hammer

A heavy club hammer is used for driving cold chisels and for a variety of demolition jobs. It is also useful for driving large masonry nails into walls.

Sledgehammer

Hire a sledgehammer if you have to break up hardcore or paving. It's also the best tool for driving stakes or fence posts into the ground, though you can make do with a club hammer if the ground is not too hard.

Sledgehammer and club hammer

Mallet

A wooden carpenter's mallet is the proper tool for driving a wood chisel. But you can use a metal hammer instead if the chisel has an impact-resistant plastic handle.

Drills

A powerful electric drill is invaluable to a builder. A cordless version is useful when you have to bore holes outdoors or in lofts and cellars that lack convenient electric sockets.

Drilling masonry for inserting wallplugs
Set the drill to hammer action and low speed. Wrap tape round the bit to mark the depth to be drilled, allowing for slightly more depth than the length of the plug. Drill the hole in stages, partly withdrawing the bit at times in order to clear the debris. To catch falling dust, tape an envelope or paper bag just below the position of the hole before starting to drill.

Power drill

Buy a good-quality power drill, plus a range of twist drills and spade bits for drilling timber. Make sure the drill has a percussion or hammer action for drilling walls.

When drilling into masonry you need to use special drill bits tipped with tungsten carbide. The smaller ones are matched to the size of standard wallplugs; and there are also much larger ones with reduced shanks that fit into a standard power-drill chuck. As the larger bits are expensive, it pays to hire them. Percussion bits are even tougher than standard masonry bits and have shatter-proof tips.

Brace

A brace is the ideal handtool for drilling large holes in timber. In addition, when fitted with a screwdriver bit, it provides the necessary leverage for inserting or extracting large woodscrews.

Saws

Every builder needs a range of saws, including an electric circular saw or a reciprocating saw for cutting heavy structural timbers. There are also some specialized saws for cutting metal and even for sawing through masonry.

Floorboard saw

Universal saw

Masonry saw

Universal saw

A single handsaw that can be used equally well for ripping solid planks lengthwise and crosscutting them to size is a useful tool to have on a building site. A saw with hardened teeth is also an asset.

Masonry saw

Masonry saws closely resemble the handsaws used for wood, but their hardened or tungsten-carbide teeth are designed to cut brick, concrete and stone.

Floorboard saw

If you prise a floorboard above its neighbours, you will be able to cut across it with an ordinary tenon saw – but the curved cutting edge of a floorboard saw makes it easier to avoid damaging the boards on either side.

Hacksaw

The hardened-steel blades of a hacksaw have fine teeth for cutting metal. Use one to cut steel concrete-reinforcing rods or small pieces of sheet metal.

All-purpose saw

An all-purpose saw is able to cut wood, metal, plastics and building boards. This type of saw is especially useful for cutting secondhand timber, which may contain nails or screws that would blunt the blade of an ordinary woodsaw.

Glazier's tools

There's little point in trying to cut glass yourself when replacing a broken window. It is better to have it cut by a professional glazier, then fit the new pane using the tools described below.

Hacking knife

A hacking knife has a heavy steel blade for chipping old putty out of window rebates in order to remove the glass. Place the point between the putty and the frame, then tap the back of the blade with a hammer.

Putty knife

The blunt blade of a putty knife is used for shaping and smoothing fresh putty. You can choose between clipped-point and straight blades, according to your personal preference.

Hacking knife

Clipped-point putty knife

Straight putty knife

SEE ALSO > Fencing 12–17, Choosing concrete blocks 23

Builder's chisels

As well as chisels for cutting and paring wood joints, you'll need some special ones when you are working on masonry.

Cold chisel

Cold chisels are made from solid-steel hexagonal-section rod. They are primarily for cutting metal bars and chopping the heads off rivets, but a builder will use one for cutting chases in plaster and brickwork or for chopping out old brick pointing.

Plugging chisel

A plugging chisel has a narrow, flat 'bit' (tip) for cutting out old or eroded pointing. It's worth having one when you need to repoint a large area of brickwork .

Bolster chisel

The wide 'bit' of a bolster chisel is designed for cutting bricks and concrete blocks. It is also useful for levering up floorboards.

Slip a plastic safety sleeve over a chisel to guard your hand against a misplaced blow from a club hammer.

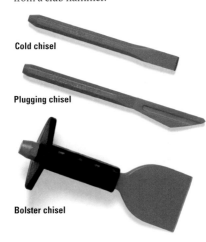

Cold chisel

Plugging chisel

Bolster chisel

Work gloves

For safety, wear strong work gloves whenever you're carrying paving slabs, concrete blocks or rough timber. The best work gloves have leather palms and fingers, although you may prefer a pair with ventilated backs for comfort in hot weather.

Digging tools

Much building work requires some kind of digging – for laying strip foundations and concrete pads, sinking rows of post holes, and so on. You probably have the basic tools in your garden shed; the others you can hire.

Pickaxe

Use a medium-weight pickaxe to break up heavily compacted soil – especially if it contains a lot of buried rubble.

Mattock

The wide blade of a mattock is ideal for breaking up heavy clay soil, and it's better than an ordinary pickaxe for ground that is riddled with tree roots.

Spade

Buy a good-quality spade for excavating soil and mixing concrete. One with a stainless-steel blade is best, but alloy steel lasts reasonably well. Choose a strong hardwood shaft split to form a D-shaped handle that is riveted with metal plates to its crosspiece. Make sure the hollow shaft socket and blade are forged in one piece.

Although square spade blades seem to be more popular, many builders prefer a round-mouth or pointed spade with a long pole handle for digging deep holes and trenches.

Shovel

You can use a spade for mixing and placing concrete or mortar, but the raised edges of a shovel retain it better.

Garden rake

Use an ordinary garden rake for spreading gravel or levelling wet concrete. Be sure to wash your rake before concrete sets on it.

Wheelbarrow

Most garden wheelbarrows aren't strong enough to cope with serious building work, which generally involves carting heavy loads of rubble and wet concrete.

Unless the tubular underframe of the wheelbarrow is rigidly strutted, you may well find that the barrow's thin metal body will distort and spill its load as you are crossing rough ground.

Check, too, that the axle is fixed securely – a cheap barrow can lose its wheel as you are tipping a load of hardcore, concrete or earth into an excavation.

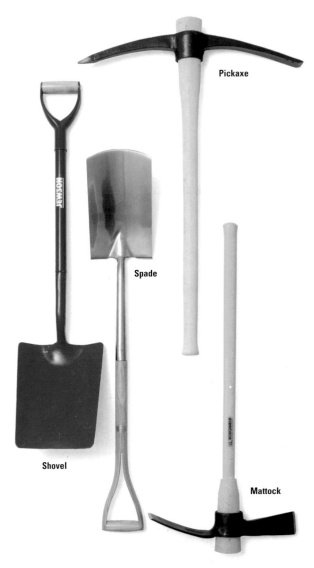

Pickaxe

Spade

Shovel

Mattock

Crowbar

A crowbar, or wrecking bar, is used for demolishing timber framework. Force the flat tip between the components and use the leverage of the long shaft to prise them apart. Choose a crowbar that has a claw at one end for removing large nails.

Slater's ripper

To replace individual slates you must cut their fixing nails without disturbing the slates overlapping them, and for this you need a slater's ripper. Pass the long hooked blade up between the slates, locate one of the hooks over the fixing nail, and pull down sharply to cut it.

● **Screwdrivers**
Most people gradually acquire an assortment of flat-tip and cross-head screwdrivers over a period of time. Alternatively, you can purchase a power screwdriver with a range of bits or buy screwdriver bits for your power drill.

● **Planes**
Most household joinery needs only skimming to leave a fairly smooth finish. A jack plane, which is a medium-size bench plane, is the most versatile general-purpose tool.

SEE ALSO > Erecting fence posts 13, Pointing brickwork 30, Constructing ponds 58

Ladders and scaffolding

Whether you need to reach guttering or require a simple step-up to paint the living-room ceiling, it is essential to use strong and stable equipment. Even for small jobs that don't justify the cost of buying ladders or scaffolding, it's advisable to hire them rather than make do. For a small outlay, you can buy accessories that make working on a ladder safer and more comfortable.

Ladder accessories

Ladder stay
A stay holds the ladder away from the wall. It is an essential piece of equipment when painting overhanging eaves and gutters – otherwise you would be forced to lean back, risking overbalancing.

Tool tray and paint-can hook
You should always support yourself with one hand on a ladder, so use a wire or bent-metal hook to hang a paint can or bucket from a rung. A clip-on tray is ideal for holding a small selection of tools.

Clip-on platform
A wide flat board that clamps onto the rungs provides a comfortable platform to stand on while working for long periods.

Stabilizers
These are bolt-on accessories that prevent the ladder from slipping and compensate for uneven ground.

Ladder accessories
This ladder has stabilizers (**1**) for uneven ground, a foot rest (**2**), a tool tray (**3**), a paint-can hook (**4**), and a stay (**5**) to hold the top away from eaves.

Ladders and towers

Lightweight metal stepladders are essential when decorating indoors. It's worth having at least one that stands about 2m (6ft 6in) high, so you can reach a ceiling without having to stand on the top step. A shorter second ladder may be more convenient for other jobs, and you can use both with scaffold boards to build a platform.

Outdoors, you will need ladders that reach up to the eaves. Double and triple extension ladders can be heavy. Some of the longer extending ladders are operated by a rope and pulley, which makes them easier to extend single-handed.

To estimate the length of ladder you are going to need, add together the ceiling heights of your house and then add at least 1m (3ft 3in) to the length – to allow for leaning the ladder at an angle and for safe access to a platform.

There are dual-purpose or even multi-purpose ladders designed to convert from stepladder to straight ladder, and some fold to make a work platform. This type of versatile ladder is a good compromise.

Sectional scaffold frames can be hired and built up to form towers at any height for decorating inside and outside. Broad feet prevent the scaffold sinking into the ground, and adjustable versions allow you to level it. Some models have locking castors that enable you to move the tower.

Towers are ideal for painting a large expanse of wall outdoors. Indoors, smaller platforms made from the same scaffold components bring high ceilings within easy reach.

Alloy stepladder **Dual-purpose ladder** **Scaffold tower** **Extending ladder**

SEE ALSO > Growing climbers 9, Pointing brickwork 30

Glossary

AGGREGATE
Particles of sand or stone mixed with cement and water to make concrete, or added to paint to make a textured finish.

APPLIANCE
A machine or device powered by electricity. or A functional piece of equipment connected to the plumbing, such as a basin, sink, bath etc.

ARRIS
The sharp edge at the meeting of two surfaces.

BALLAST
Naturally occurring sand and gravel mix used as aggregate for making concrete.

BALUSTER
One of a set of posts supporting a stair handrail.

BALUSTRADE
The protective barrier alongside a staircase or landing.

BASECOAT
A flat coat of paint over which a decorative glaze is applied.

BATT
A short cut length of glass-fibre or mineral-fibre insulant.

BATTEN
A narrow strip of wood.

BATTER
The slope of the face of a wall that leans backwards or tapers from bottom to top.

BLIND
To cover with sand.

BLOWN
Broken away, as when a layer of cement rendering has parted from a wall.

BORE
The hollow part of a pipe or tube. or To drill a hole.

BUTTERCOAT
The top layer of cement render.

CASING
The timber lining of a door or window opening.

CATENARY WIRE
A length of wire cable suspended horizontally between two points.

CAVITY WALL
A wall made of two separate, parallel masonry skins with an air space between them.

CHASE
A groove cut in masonry or plaster to accept pipework or an electrical cable. or To cut or channel such grooves.

CIRCUIT
A complete path through which an electric current can flow.

CONDUCTOR
A component, usually a length of wire, along which an electric current will pass.

COUNTERBORE
To cut a hole that allows the head of a bolt or screw to lie below a surface. or Such a hole.

COUNTERSINK
To cut a tapered recess that allows the head of a screw to lie flush with a surface. or The tapered recess itself.

CUP
To bend as a result of shrinkage, specifically across the width of a piece of wood.

DAMP-PROOF COURSE
A layer of impervious material that prevents moisture rising from the ground into the walls of a building.

DAMP-PROOF MEMBRANE
A layer of impervious material that prevents moisture rising through a concrete floor.

DATUM POINT
The point from which measurements are taken.

DPC
See Damp-proof course.

DPM
See Damp-proof membrane.

DRIP GROOVE
A groove cut or moulded in the underside of a windowsill to prevent rainwater running back to the wall.

EAVES
The edges of a roof that project beyond the walls.

EFFLORESCENCE
A white powdery deposit caused by soluble salts migrating to the surface of a wall or ceiling.

END GRAIN
The surface of wood exposed after cutting across the fibres.

EXTENSION
A room or rooms added to an existing building.

EXTENSION LEAD
A length of electrical flex for temporarily connecting the short permanent flex of an appliance to a wall socket.

FACE EDGE
In woodworking, the surface planed square to the face side.

FACE SIDE
In woodworking, the flat planed surface from which other dimensions and angles are measured and worked.

FALL
A downward slope.

FASCIA
A strip of wood that covers the ends of rafters and to which external guttering is fixed.

FEATHER
To wear away or smooth an edge until it is undetectable.

FENCE
An adjustable guide to keep the cutting edge of a tool a set distance from the edge of a workpiece.

FLASHING
A weatherproof junction between a roof and a wall or chimney, or between one roof and another.

FLUTE
A rounded concave groove.

FOOTING
A narrow concrete foundation for a wall.

FRASS
Powdered wood produced by the activity of woodworm.

FROG
The angled depression in one face of some housebricks.

FURRING BATTENS
See Furring strips.

FURRING STRIPS
Parallel strips of wood fixed to a wall or ceiling to provide a framework for attaching panels.

GALVANIZED
Covered with a protective coating of zinc.

GOING
The horizontal measurement between the top and bottom risers of a stair or the depth of one tread.

GRAIN
The general direction of wood fibres. or The pattern produced on the surface of timber by cutting through the fibres. See also End grain and Short grain.

GROOVE
A long narrow channel cut in plaster or wood in the general direction of the grain. or To cut such channels.

GULLET
The notch formed between two saw teeth.

HARDCORE
Broken bricks or stones used to form a sub-base below paving, foundations etc.

HARDWOOD
Timber from deciduous trees.

HEAD
The height of the surface of water above a specific point, used as a measurement of pressure – for example, a head of 2m (6ft). or The top horizontal member of a wooden frame.

HEAVE
An upward swelling of ground caused by excessive moisture.

HELICAL
Spiral shaped.

HOGGIN
A fine ballast, usually with a clay content, used to form a sub-base for concrete pads or paving.

HONE
To sharpen a cutting edge.

HOUSING
A long narrow channel cut across the general direction of wood grain to form part of a joint.

INSULATION
Materials used to reduce the transmission of heat or sound.or Nonconductive material surrounding electrical wires or connections to prevent the passage of electricity.

JAMB
The vertical side member of a doorframe or window frame.

JOIST
A horizontal wooden or metal beam (such as an RSJ) used to support a structure such as a floor, ceiling or wall.

KERF
The groove cut by a saw.

KNOTTING
Sealer, made from shellac, that prevents wood resin bleeding through a surface finish.

KNURLED
Impressed with a series of fine grooves designed to improve the grip, for instance a knurled knob or handle.

LATH AND PLASTER
A method of finishing a timber-frame wall or ceiling. Narrow strips of wood are nailed to the studs or joists to provide a supporting framework for plaster or tiles.

LEAD
A stepped section of brickwork or blockwork built at each end of a wall to act as a guide to the height of the intermediate coursing.

LINTEL
A horizontal beam used to support the wall over a door or window opening.

MARINE PLYWOOD
Exterior-grade plywood.

MASTIC
A nonsetting compound used to seal joints.

MICROPOROUS
See Moisture-vapour permeable.

MITRE
A joint formed between two pieces of wood by cutting bevels of equal angle at the ends of each piece. or To cut the joint.

MOISTURE-VAPOUR PERMEABLE
Used to describe a finish that allows moisture to escape from timber, allowing it to dry out, while protecting the wood from rainwater or damp. The same term is used to describe a paint that can be applied over new plaster without sealing in the moisture.

MONO-PITCH ROOF
A roof that slopes in one direction only.

MORTISE
A rectangular recess cut in timber to receive a matching tongue or tenon.

MOUSE
A small weight used to help pass a line through a narrow vertical space.

NEEDLE
A stout wooden beam used with props to support the section of a wall above an opening prior to the installation of an RSJ or lintel.

OXIDIZE
To form a layer of metal oxide, as in rusting.

PARE
To remove fine shavings from wood with a chisel.

PENETRATING OIL
A thin lubricant that will seep between corroded components and ease them apart.

PILOT HOLE
A small-diameter hole drilled prior to the insertion of a woodscrew to act as a guide for its thread.

PINCH ROD
A wooden batten used to gauge the width of a frame or opening.

POINT LOAD
The concentration of forces on a very small area.

PRIMER
The first coat of a paint system applied to protect wood or metal. A wood primer reduces the absorption of subsequent undercoats and top coats. A metal primer prevents corrosion.

PROFILE
The outline or contour of an object.

PROTECTIVE MULTIPLE EARTH
A system of electrical wiring in which the neutral part of the circuit is used to take earth-leakage current to earth.

PURLIN
A horizontal beam that provides intermediate support for rafters or sheet roofing.

RAFTER
One of a set of parallel sloping beams that form the main structural element of a roof.

RATCHET
A device that permits movement in one direction only by restricting the reversal of a toothed wheel or rack.

REBATE
A stepped rectangular recess along the edge of a workpiece, usually forming part of a joint. or To cut such recesses.

RENDER
A thin layer of cement-based mortar applied to exterior walls to provide a protective finish. Sometimes fine stone aggregate is embedded in the mortar. or To apply such mortar.

REVEAL
The vertical side of an opening in a wall.

RISER
The vertical part of a step.

RSJ (ROLLED STEEL JOIST)
A steel beam, usually with a cross section in the form of a capital letter I.

RUB JOINT
Glued wood rubbed together and held by suction until it sets.

RUBBER
A pad of cotton wool wrapped in soft cloth used to apply stain, shellac polish etc.

SCRATCHCOAT
The bottom layer of cement.

SCREED
A thin layer of mortar applied to give a smooth surface to concrete etc. or A shortened name for screed batten.

SCREED BATTEN
A thin strip of wood fixed to a surface to act as a guide to the thickness of an application of plaster or render.

SETT
A small rectangular paving block.

SHORT GRAIN
When the general direction of wood fibres lies across a narrow section of timber.

SILL
The lowest horizontal member of a frame that surrounds a door or window. or The lowest horizontal member of a stud partition.

SLEEPER WALL
A low masonry wall that serves as an intermediate support for ground-floor joists.

SOAKAWAY
A pit filled with rubble or gravel into which water is drained.

SOFFIT
The underside of part of a building such as an archway or the eaves etc.

SOFTWOOD
Timber from coniferous trees.

SPALLING
Flaking of the outer face of masonry caused by expanding moisture in icy conditions.

STOPPER
A wood filler made in colours to match various kinds of timber.

SUBSIDENCE
A sinking of the ground caused by the shrinkage of excessively dry soil.

TAMP
To pack down firmly with repeated blows.

TENON
A projecting tongue on the end of a piece of wood that fits into a corresponding mortise.

THINNER
A solvent, such as turpentine, used to dilute paint or varnish.

TOP COAT
The outer layer of a paint system.

TREAD
The horizontal part of a step.

UNDERCOAT
A layer or layers of paint used to obliterate the colour of a primer and build a protective body of paint before applying a top coat.

VAPOUR BARRIER
A layer of impervious material that prevents the passage of moisture-laden air.

WALL PLATE
A horizontal timber member placed along the top of a wall to support the ends of joists and spread their load.

WALL TIE
A strip of metal or bent wire used to bind sections of masonry together.

WANEY EDGE
A natural wavy edge on a plank. It may still be covered by bark.

WEATHERED
Showing signs of exposure to the weather. or Sloped so as to shed rainwater.

WEEP HOLE
A small hole at the base of a cavity wall that allows absorbed water to drain to the outside.

WORKPIECE
An object in the process of being shaped, produced or otherwise worked on. Sometimes referred to simply as the 'work'.

Index